RED HILL

The miners' strike of 1984–5 was one of the longest and most bitter in Britain's history, and polarised arguments and emotions with more force than any other industrial dispute for years. Six months after it ended, Tony Parker went to the north-east of England to discover the feelings and thoughts of a community around a coal-mine scheduled to be closed, but where there was still hope that the National Coal Board might reprieve it.

Talking with those on both sides of the dispute – miners, their wives, Union officials, policemen, shopkeepers, young people, Coal Board officials, schoolteachers and many others – he offers a truthful and moving portrait of life in a coalfield community today.

Also by the same author,
and available from Coronet:

SOLDIER, SOLDIER

About the author

Tony Parker was born in Manchester in 1923,
and worked underground in a coal-mine during
the 1939–45 war. He is the author of many
books, including THE COURAGE OF HIS
CONVICTIONS, THE UNKNOWN CITIZEN,
THE TWISTING LANE, LIGHTHOUSE,
THE PEOPLE OF PROVIDENCE and
SOLDIER, SOLDIER.

Tony Parker lives in Suffolk and he and his wife
have five grown-up children.

Red Hill
A Mining Community

Tony Parker

CORONET BOOKS
Hodder and Stoughton

Copyright © Tony Parker 1986

First published in Great Britain in 1986 by William Heinemann Limited

Coronet edition 1988

British Library C.I.P.

Parker, Tony
   Red Hill: a mining community.
   1. Coal strike, Great Britain, 1984–1985
   —Personal narratives
   I. Title
   331.89'2822334'0922
   HD5365.M6152 1984

ISBN 0-340-42365-X

Printed and bound in Great Britain for Hodder and Stoughton Paperbacks, a division of Hodder and Stoughton Limited, Mill Road, Dunton Green, Sevenoaks, Kent TN13 2YA (Editorial Office: 47 Bedford Square, London WC1B 3DP) by Richard Clay Limited, Bungay, Suffolk. Photoset by Rowland Phototypesetting Limited, Bury St Edmunds, Suffolk.

For John
stepson and friend
with love

In the Falklands, we had to fight the enemy without. Here the enemy is within, and it is more difficult to fight, and more dangerous to liberty.

The Rt Hon Margaret Thatcher, MP, Prime Minister
(Speech to the 1922 Committee, 20 July 1984)

People are now discovering the price of insubordination and insurrection. And boy, are we going to make it stick.

Ian MacGregor, Chairman of the National Coal Board
(Interview in the Sunday Telegraph, 10 March 1985)

Contents

Preface

Red Hill is not the real name of the coal mine, nor of the village around it: and in most cases I have not used people's real names in order to obscure their identity, usually at their request.

But it is a real pit, they are real people, and this is what they said.

TP

Part I

Head down and fast as I can away
John and Moira Potter

Just one of your ordinary people like
Bill Barrymore

The good old solid Union man
Geoff Danson

No chance of a football life for me
Harry Hartley

It's very very quiet now down the pit
Norman Lane

My long and happy retirement
Bernard Wilkinson

I'd say it was a place full of laughter
Tom Day

Not all honey and spice
George Driver
Cliff Marshall
Alan Whitfield
Gary Neil

Head down and fast as I can away
John and Moira Potter

On the hillside above the village, the long terrace of little two-up two-down houses was identical with the terrace facing it on the opposite side of the street: and the street was identical with the next one running parallel with it, with the one after that and with the one after that. Some of the houses had had their windows modernised, and some had brightly painted front doors – scarlet, purple, yellow, green. Otherwise they were all the same: and solidly built of dark heavy stone. Behind each was a uniform small backyard. His was number 41 Rope Street.

– Me, every day when I leave the pit, it's head down and fast as I can away. The end of the shift is the end of the shift, know what I mean? I don't hang about, I like to get home here to the wife and the bairns as quick as I can, shut my front door and have a bath, and put my feet up in front of the fire with my slippers on and relax. I'm forty-nine, Moira's forty-eight, we've a boy Darren seventeen and a girl Angie who's thirteen. Darren's left school and's at college doing his higher maths and we hope he'll go on from there and go into engineering or something of that sort. Angie, well we don't know yet what she'll do, at the moment she's all for being a nurse, but she's young and she could change her mind. Kids do don't they eh?

This house we live in here is a Coal Board house, we get it at a very small rent, two pounds something a week. A couple of years or so back we inquired about buying it, but they told us they're pulling them all down in the next few years. There was talk they were going to build new ones further up the hill, but I suppose all that depends on whether they keep Red Hill open or not. If we have to move out of here we'll get a council house I suppose. The wife's quite keen on us going to Peterlee: I wouldn't mind where it was, so long as it was handy for me to get to my work. I've got a car: it's a five-year-old Cortina, a bit of a banger but it does me. You have to have a car, especially in the winter or when you're on late turn like.

Being a miner, I'd say it's not a bad life. When I first went in the pit it was straight from school, I never thought about doing nothing else or going nowhere else. My father before me had been here at Red Hill all his life, and two of his brothers my uncles the same. He'd three girls and me: I was his only son, so I think he'd have liked for me to do something else. But the pit's a secure job, least it was those days: anyway you always felt if you didn't like it you could try something else. Now it's different mind, there's not the recruiting: but for those who are in it already the Board has said every man who still wants a job, he'll be able to have one. I know a lot of men who've taken transfers. Or if you don't, you get redundancy money. I don't think I need think about redundancy for a few years for me, that's something'll be to consider for the future. If they do close Red Hill, I shall have choice: redundancy or transfer and if I chose transfer I'll be offered a couple of alternatives. I don't much mind where I go. They say Waddell Moor's a pit with a good future for several more years yet, so I should think it'll probably be there. Mind you if they start messing me about after that, then I'm fairly definite in my own mind I'll leave the industry. I'm the sort of person likes to be settled. I'm a trained welder so I wouldn't even have to stay in the mines.

So yes I'd say we'd had a fairly decent life like: we're not rolling in money but we're comfortable enough. We're simple people, we don't ask for a great lot of luxuries or nothing of that sort. We have our house and our holiday once a year and that does us nicely. For our holiday we always go a bit of a way further down along the coast here to that big caravan park you might have seen, Sunland, yes: we like it there. We're not ones for always gadding off to Spain and all that sort of thing you know: it's very expensive there, first going and then when you get there

everyone trying to sell you souvenirs and make money out
of you. And you've got to be very careful about what sort
of thing you eat. From what I can make out from people
I know who've been, when they get there most of them
eat in their own hotels and stick to the English food that's
served them, just to be on the safe side. Well myself I
don't see a lot of point in that, paying a lot of money to
go to a foreign country and then eat exactly the same sort
of thing you can make for yourself here at home. And
paying hundreds of pounds for the privilege of doing it,
I think that's crackers. Anyway, the wife doesn't like
aeroplanes so we've never bothered.

Anyway there's no particular other country in the world
I specially want to go and see. I think old England's the
best; it's got the best people in the world, so why should
you want to go anywhere else eh? Angie was talking just
a few weeks ago about there's going to be a school trip to
France. Next year I think it is. She says she'd like to go
on it just so in order she can have a look. We'll probably
let her go, because I think she'd feel out of it if her other
school mates were going and she wasn't. But I've warned
her, I've said to her it's going to cost a fair bit of money,
so I hope she won't be disappointed in it. Mind you, travel,
I don't think myself you need it. With what you get
nowadays on the television, that's like a window on the
whole world isn't it? Every night you see all sorts of foreign
countries that you never knew anything about at all, you'd
never even heard of. But I've never seen not one so far
that looked to be a patch on our country. Most of what
you hear about everywhere is famine and starvation and
wars and killing and things of that sort. So thank God
for Great Britain eh, we don't have things like that do
we?

I mean though don't get me wrong, I'm not one of those
narrow-minded people who all he does is wave the Union
Jack around and he won't see anything good in anyone
else at all. Some of the other countries, I do admit they
can teach us things. Specially say in football or things of

that sort, I mean the Brazilians in the World Cup they were a real treat to watch eh? But then another time you see all the dirt and poverty they live in: horrible conditions, you wouldn't want to swap places with them not for all the tea in China.

Altogether, the wife and I've had a very very full life all along. We've been blessed with good health which is the main thing, and our children have grown up to be everything anyone could ever want. Darren's a very clever boy, a bright lad: I'm glad he's got no thoughts himself of coal mining. Mind you he might one day end up in the industry but as an engineer say. I think he's got the possibility of doing all sorts of things if he puts his mind to it. Being away at college is something I think's very good for a young man, it opens his eyes and gives him chances. If Angie follows in his footsteps in her own way in her own time, we shall be very proud then. But even if she doesn't the wife says no matter what, she's got a nice home and a good husband and two lovely bairns, and no one could ask for more out of life than that. She's a person who's perfectly happy and content with her home and her family is the wife: not like some of these women you hear about these days, who all they want to do is complain about what a hard time they have and how unhappy they are. She's been a good wife to me and a good mother to the children she has. In return we've all of us always been very full of gratitude for her for all she's done for us. Mother's Day's always a big day in our house. It's been our habit for years now, we don't let her do nothing at all on that day, it's the one day in the year that's hers. She gets her tea brought to her up in bed, and a nice big bunch of flowers. She's not allowed to do any cooking, we have a real spread from the Chinese takeaway or that other place what's it called, where you get the chicken in boxes from. So there's no washing-up either, and she just sits all day in this chair here and we wait on her hand and foot. We've always made a point of it: I think children should be brought up to appreciate their mother. I do, and a lot of them don't get it nowadays: but ours have always had it told to them, your best friend is your mother.

I'd say all in all that that's about it, as far as our life here in this house is concerned. I don't have any actual what you might call hobbies of my own, except I enjoy making things for the house. I put up those shelves there, I made that fixture in the corner which we call our cocktail bar, I put up those shelves you saw all around the kitchen when we were making the cups of coffee. I think a woman has to have the best kitchen that it's possible, with all the latest in the modern gadgets. It's the heart of her home, and it's of benefit to everybody: that's her working place, she cooks us lovely meals, makes cakes, irons our clothes, everything. So to my mind she deserves to have the very best of everything there is, and always to work in a really nice environment. Next time you come you must get her to show you some of the things she's got in her cupboards: best tea services, dinner sets, if there's anything at all we're short of as a family, for entertaining other people or for ourselves, I shall be very surprised for you to be able to think of it. A really good home and a really good life, that would just about sum it up.

– The wife's gone over to her sister's at Peterlee tonight. She says she was sorry not to meet you this time, but her sister's got the flu. And with three small children, well so she's gone to give her a hand with things. It's typical of her to do something like that, she's a person who won't stand by if she sees someone else is in trouble. She says to give you her good wishes and she hopes next time you come she'll be here. She's made some sandwiches for us which she's left on top of the fridge: we'll have some coffee eh and go on with our chat. A lot of people here in Red Hill, they mostly spend their evening times down in the clubs. Drinking, playing darts and snooker and that. Talk their heads off with one another all night long. I'm more of a quiet sort myself, I don't usually speak unless I've got something to say. I'll be friendly all right, but I don't see no sense in sitting round putting the world to rights, or telling dirty jokes. And sometimes an argument can blow up, especially if someone's had one or two more pints than he should. I think the best thing's to keep yourself to yourself as far as possible. I think there's a lot of people make themselves unhappy by always complaining about things. And they're not things that can be altered anyway. I think you should make the best of what you've got and be thankful for it: I think a lot more people would be a lot more happy if they did.

Last time you said when you came round tonight you'd like me to talk to you about the strike. So right, and well to me that was a very good example indeed of what I've just been saying. To my mind you see we should never have had the strike, because it wasn't nothing else but a complete waste of time. It brought a lot of hardship and a lot of suffering to a whole lot of people, and it got no one anywhere at the end of it. I think it was a terrible thing: all it was was an example of people looking round for something to make themselves unhappy about, the sort of people I've just been talking about.

I don't think the strike was for any proper reason at all. I supported the strikes we had in 1972 and 1974 because these were to get us more money basically. I think that's what you should strike for, more money if you're not getting your fair wages in comparison with somebody else. But I don't see how you can strike to try and keep your job in a pit, where that pit's not economic for them to keep on producing coal from. That's what they said it was all about. I think that's bloody ridiculous. It's like having a strike to keep a supermarket open, when it hasn't got no goods for sale on its shelves. It wouldn't make sense for the staff to go on strike and demand they should be allowed to stay there and just stand around all day with nothing to sell would it? The bloody strike was just the bloody same.

But I'm not one of those who'll tell you it was all just part of a plot by Arthur Scargill to bring down the

Government. I think he's a cleverer man than that: well he has to be hasn't he, or he wouldn't have got where he's got? But to try and get all his Union members to come out on strike when he's saying all he wants is that they should all have jobs, well that's an arse over tip if ever I heard one. It'd make more sense to tell them all to stay in the pits and work twenty-four hours a day rather than tell them all to not work.

I'm not one either who'll try to tell you the Government had some deep-laid plan to close down the coal industry. It's the Coal Board who are the industry's managers, and it's up to them to run it in the way they think is the most profitable. That's what they're paid to do, that's their job: so it can't be in their interests to close it all down altogether can it? But if they've gone into something and decide it's not worth the expense of keeping a pit in production any longer, I don't see what else they could be expected to do but to close that pit down. The Board've said all along they'll pay redundancies to those who want to leave, or find jobs in other pits for those who want to transfer. That suits me. I believe them. I've worked for the Coal Board all my life: I don't think they've been bad employers, in fact in most cases I think they've been very good, they helped me get my training and all the rest of it. They've certainly spent millions of pounds improving the working conditions in pits for the likes of thousands of men. That hasn't brought them any extra profit, it's cost them a lot of money. That's something I think a lot of people don't take into account sufficiently.

How do you mean? Well to answer your question honestly, I'll tell you: I've never been to a Union meeting ever in my whole life. Like I told you the other night, I'm not a person who has much time for talk. And that's all that the Union meetings are, just talk, from all I hear about them. They pass their resolutions and all the rest of it, but I think they're all just playing a game, sort of to make themselves feel important. For those who like that sort of thing, fair enough: but for people like me who don't, all I can say is leave them alone to get on with it. There's been some bloody ridiculous incidents in my time at the pit, the Union saying this man can't do that little thing because it's some other man's job: they'll even bring the whole pit to a stop because of some stupid thing like that. All that's nonsense to me, I say all I want's just to be left alone and get on with the job.

No, I wouldn't scab though, oh no. It's as much as your life's worth. If the Union says we're on strike brother, then we're on strike. I stopped work when they told me to and I didn't start again until the day that they told me to either. They'd make your life hell when you went back to work afterwards if you'd scabbed, it's not worth it. The strike wasn't easy as far as the money was concerned, there was nothing coming in: but we had a fair bit we'd put by over the years, so we had to use some of that for living on. My father and mother, and the wife's father and mother who're Scottish people, they were all very generous and they helped us out. There've been times when we've been able to do little things for them, like giving them a caravan holiday with us and that sort of thing, that they've appreciated at the time: so when it came we were up against it we didn't have to ask them, they helped us out. I've always said when we were back at work we'd start to pay some of it back: I've not been able to start doing that yet up to now, but I will do. I've every intention of keeping the promise, I don't like to be in a position where I'm obligated to someone, I never have.

I think the Union's all right, but there's a time and place for it. I suppose, when you think about it, it wouldn't have grown up if there hadn't been need for it. But that was a long time ago you know, before my time. You read in books and places how in the bad old days they used to have women and children working down the mines, men getting choked to death with the coal dust and all the rest of it. But those days are over and gone, and the Union did its job and got a betterment of conditions. I don't think it's got much to do with things as they are in pits nowadays.

The loudest mouths in it are always the ones you feel they'd start an argument with anybody over anything at any time, just for the sheer pleasure of it. I don't reckon a lot to them myself.

Anyway, next time the wife eh? No, she'll be pleased to.

– No no, I'm a Highland lassie, can you not tell? When I first came to Red Hill with John he said everyone'd have to have a phrase book to understand what I was saying. More than twenty years ago that was, I hope I haven't lost all my accent, I'd like to keep a wee bit. But it works the other way round too: when I go back to Edinburgh to see my mother and father there's people up there I used to know when I was younger, they say all my accent's gone and anyone'd think I wasn't Scottish at all.

Well it was funny how me and John came to meet. He was up in Scotland on his holidays with one of his pals, on one of those coach tours, you know? We met in an Edinburgh dance hall. It sounds romantic when I tell it to people like that, but it wasn't: I was a table waitress working there and he started being real cheeky to me. I told him if he didn't mind what he was saying I'd give him one, I was, I was really cross about it. And then the next night what should he do but he come back again. Only this time on his own without his pal: and he said he'd come back to apologise to me. He said he liked my spirit, the way I'd spoken up to him the night before, would I like to come out with him the night after that so's he could make it up to me? I could see he wasn't like I'd thought he was, but I told him I wasn't going to agree to go out with him till he'd been in the dance hall a few times more. He said he couldn't do that, because he was on this coach tour. And then he told me he'd let them go off without him, up into the lochs for two days, but he'd have to join up with them again when they came back, so he could go home down here. He'd done all that, missed seeing the scenery and everything, found himself a cheap hotel he'd had to pay extra for, stayed behind in Edinburgh without his pal, all because he wanted to see me again. Any girl'd have to have a hard heart not to be nice to someone like that wouldn't she?

After he'd gone back we wrote, then he came up to Edinburgh again, I came down here, and I think it was only about six months and we were married. Everyone said it was too quick, well anyway my mother did I remember: but I've never regretted it, he's been a good husband to me and a good father to our two bairns. So that's really all there is to my life story, very simple and straightforward and we've not had half the troubles lots of other people have had. I'm a firm religious person myself and I'd tell anyone, we've a lot to thank Almighty God for in our lives. And that John's health's stayed good and he's never had no accidents, that's another thing. But he works on the bank, that's what they call the surface: he has done for years, he's in one of the maintenance shops. He's a skilled man at his welding trade so they keep him there, he doesn't go down underground anymore.

That's why the strike was very difficult for us you see, because John didn't have to stop at the pit, he could have gone off and got a job somewhere else. He could have gone anywhere he liked really, anyone'd have been glad to have him. Many a time I said to him why didn't he leave, he could get a job right out of the mines, in Peterlee even: that'd be a nice place to live too. It was ridiculous for us to be like we were, not knowing where we were going to get money to live on from, not knowing when we were going to get it either. But he said it'd look bad, he'd have to stick it out.

I didn't understand that, and to tell you the truth I still don't. I think it was his father was at the back of it, he's always a big Union man is John's father, even though he's retired. John doesn't have any time for all that sort of thing himself though, he likes to stay at home and watch the telly. Or his hobby, which is making things for the house: cupboards and shelves, anything you can think of. He made that: and that, and that. I think it's another thing he could do for a living if he wanted, some people have it in their hands naturally don't they, to be able to make things? We've got a caravan and he's fitted out the inside of that from top to bottom and it is, it's really lovely. Not a caravan you can go moving about in, no: it's fixed on a site, it's like a sort of chalet-home, we just use it for the summer. Sometimes I've wished we did have one of the other sort yes, it'd be nice to go touring round. Perhaps in a few years when the bairns are off our hands. Then we could even go up and tour round the Highlands, John's still never seen them. Mind you, one place I'd like to go for a holiday, just once, is somewhere abroad. My sister and her husband, they go nearly every year for their holidays to Greece, they say it's lovely. But John's not much for that sort of thing, he says he'd sooner stop in this country because of the food. Greece would be nice though, just one year.

Still I don't want you to think I'm a complaining sort of person, I'm not: well I think I'm not, I hope I'm not. You can't have had the sort of life I've had without being very thankful for it. You see all these plays and things nowadays they have on television, and most of them they're all such unhappy people aren't they? What was that one the other night, did you see it, there was this young woman, she'd got a nice house and a lovely baby, and she ran away from it all to be on her own because she said it was all boring. I said to John I said 'Well, honestly, some people don't know they're born.' I think there's a lot of people like that. Should we have a cup of tea?

– Well where the strike was concerned, it was very awkward for us like I said. But still, we got through and we kept cheerful, that was the main thing. My parents were very very good, they helped us out over things with money they sent us from time to time. I don't mean we asked for it or anything of that sort, but you know just now and again: it helped us get a few little extras once in a while.

And we had got a little bit of our own put away for a rainy day. We always said we wouldn't ever touch it unless we had to, but the strike was a rainy day wasn't it, so that helped us through.

And I don't suppose it matters saying this, I expect John'll have told you himself about it. But there were one or two people asked him to do things for them as well: he'd plenty of time on his hands, so he went and put in new windows for them, or kitchen cupboards and bedroom wardrobes, that sort of thing. I mean we both felt it was better than him just sitting around the house doing nothing all day: he might as well be doing things for other people, and if it helped out on the money side of things a bit well so much the better.

So yes all in all we didn't do too badly through the strike, not one way and another. We kept our heads above water, let's put it like that. But we were very glad when it was over though, and everyone could get back to work and forget about it. It'll be a shame if they do close down Red Hill like they're talking about, after all that: but if it's got to be then it's got to be, that's what John says.

I think the same. I leave all that to the men, I don't go in for politics myself, I don't really understand it. All the way through John said he thought the strike was stupid. He's in the mines, he's been in coal mining all his life: I think if he says that, he's someone who knows what he's talking about so I leave it to him. They said it was about work and closing pits down didn't they, but I don't know, none of it means much to me. It's not something that means much to me. It's not something that affects us really, I don't think John's ever going to be short of work of some kind. And I certainly didn't hold with all that shouting and screaming and fighting you saw all the time on the television. I thought it was dreadful. We didn't have much of that round here I'm glad to say. I don't know what most people thought about it, we're people who keep ourselves to ourselves mainly, we don't mix in much with other people. We go once a week to Newcastle shopping because things are cheaper there, but apart from that we don't really go out, and not socialising.

The women who had what they call the 'Support Groups' do you mean? I don't know any of those, I think they were mostly from over the other side more. I think a couple of them did come round once knocking on the door saying there was going to be a meeting and would I like to come. But I told them I wasn't interested. I mean if you want to do it I suppose it's all right, but I think some of them neglected their homes and families if you want my honest opinion about it. I saw some of them on the television one night, they were making a big lot of noise. I don't think that's the way to behave if you want to do things.

To me it's your husband and your family first, they're what's important. Don't interefere with other people, that's my motto: you live your own life, and let other people get on with living theirs.

*Just one of your ordinary people like
Bill Barrymore*

– Oh I'm a man with problems at the moment I'd say. One of us bairns is not well, she's in hospital but it doesn't seem they can put their finger on what is wrong with her. Something with her chest and it's worrying. The other two older ones are all right, but it's only natural with it going on and on it's getting the wife down. Most nights she stays over in the hospital, a three-year-old needs her mam eh? But it's wearing for her what with that and a part-time job and looking after me and Esther and Lesley into the bargain, it's a lot. I'm on the six o'clock morning shift this turn, so she tries to get home here for half-past five.

If they do close Red Hill pit next year like they say, we'll not know where we are worse than ever eh? Sometimes I think we're having more than our share of problems. But then you hear what someone else is having to put up with, you think well what am I complaining about, things must be much worse for them.

A broad-shouldered long-legged man in jeans and a red and green zippered cardigan, he stretched his feet out towards the banked-up coal fire as he lay back almost horizontally in his armchair. His voice was quiet. He spoke with long pauses, frowning sometimes at the flames as though looking in them for his thoughts.

– I'm different to what I was say three years ago. Very different. I'm thirty-six but sometimes I can tell you, I do, I feel like a hundred. A funny time of your life thirty-six is, you don't know whether to look on it as the end of the beginning, or the beginning of the end like. I'd not say I was a good talker at the best of times, I've never known properly how to put things into words you see. And I'm more confused now in my thoughts than ever. But begin at the beginning would be the best eh, yeh.

Well I left school at fifteen, and went straight into Red Hill pit. I've been there ever since. My dad was a miner at Red Hill all his life, and his father before him, and I think his father before him. So it's what you might say our family pit like. I'd uncles there too.

There was always the knowledge that Red Hill was where I was going to go. My dad didn't want me to, I think most miners in those days didn't want their sons to go down the mine. But then in those days the employment situation was better, you see. I think what he wanted was for me to try something else first, see if I couldn't get into a better job. I had a brother older than me, and he did. He went into the merchant navy for a while but then he came back and went in Red Hill. He was the one moved a few years ago to the Yorkshire coalfield, and was at Cortonwood.

For my dad you see, the pit was what you might call a last option for me. He had a notion I might do better: but if that didn't work out then there was the job in the pit waiting. But me, I didn't look at it like that. I was happy, there was nothing else I wanted to do. I wanted to work in Red Hill pit. This is the area all my family is, my school mates were down the pit or going to go down it. I didn't want to go off out into the world somewhere to seek my fortune. I didn't look at it like that.

If the pit's your own community and that community's the only one you've been in all your life, you look at it that here you're in amongst your own so that's where you want to stay. This is why like everyone else, the only one word for it is I hate and fear the idea we might lose Red Hill. If they close the pit they're closing down my life. And not just mine mind, but everyone else's who works there, who lives in the village here round the pit. When I said it's our family pit, I'm not the only one saying that, there's another eight hundred families all saying the same thing. All our working lives we've been together, same work mates, same people, same community. When they talk of shutting us down they pay no attention to that eh? It's not important, not in the way they look at it. Close down the pit, let the men who worked there go their different ways. Some retire early, some take redundancy, some transfer to other places. Fuck the community eh, fuck the people, they've got to adjust themselves, that's the only way to run the mines. Community? Who cares about that? I'll not be the only one who tells you what a day that'll be if they close Red Hill. We're fighting it, we're going to do everything we can think of to keep it going: because otherwise it'll just be somebody closing a book and saying 'Well that's the end of that.'

I wouldn't want to take a transfer myself. I wouldn't want to work at any other pit I wouldn't, for a whole lot of different reasons. The main one is I wouldn't be happy working in any other pit. Wherever they are, the men there'll be good men, I'm not saying anything about that. But they've got their mates naturally just like as I've got mine: and it'd take a long time to work in with them. It wouldn't be the same place as here, and there'd be a lot of travelling to another place to work. Here it's only just along the road see, and it's home.

What I would do is take redundancy, then try for another job somewhere else in my own trade. In the pit I'm an electrician. And so the way I'm thinking at present, I'd try for an electrician's job somewhere else, not in a mine. God knows where because there'd be lots of men similar to myself trying to find themselves new jobs out of the mines as well. But definitely I wouldn't want to go to some other pit. The Coal Board says there'll be jobs for everyone that wants them. Well so there might be, but I don't want one of them jobs in another pit thanks very much, not after what they've done to us. You can't rely on them.

The wife and I've talked over a time or two whether I should try and set up in a business of my own. We've talked it over time and again actually, sometimes I think we've been talking it over for the past two years. Only there are all sorts of problems attached to it eh? You read in the papers every day of small businesses going broke don't you, and if that happened what little bit of money we had would be lost as well as everything else. It's a big risk. When you've got a family like we have, three children, you have to give it a lot of thought before you go and do something of that sort.

Our house we live in, this one, we're buying it from the council see. When they were encouraging us to do things of that sort, the Government weren't telling us we could well end up buying a council house but there'd be no job for us, oh no. And the lasses: one twelve, one six and one three. Their friends are all here aren't they, they all live round about here. So if I were to go and get a job somewhere else it'd mean they'd have to pull their roots up too. Going to live in a new place, selling this house, trying to get another one . . . it's all a lot of problems eh, a big lot of problems. The wife gets depressed, I worry, the kids're unsettled: perhaps we shouldn't worry as much as we do but that's the sort of people we are. And the wife's family, they all live round here as well: going away'd be a complete break for her with everyone.

I'm a working man, I'm not frightened of hard work, I've worked hard all my life: but if they close down Red Hill . . . Well I do, I find it very hard to think about, never mind talk about, I do. I don't want to face it. I sometimes wake up in the night and I think Christ what'll I do if they do?

Well I fancy a beer I do, what about you?

– Last time I got a bit down didn't I eh, yeh. It's changed me you know, the strike and all the uncertainty afterwards. It's like you're living in uncertainty, waiting to hear what's going to happen to you, not being able to do anything that'll have any influence. Kites without wind, that's what we are. You know there's nothing you can do, and that's

not a nice feeling. It's waking up to the fact that halfway
through my life all the things I thought I'd been doing
hadn't really meant anything. I wasn't a brain person, I
was a hard manual worker, a physical worker, I've never
been a shirker. I'd worked, and worked hard. All I'd
wanted to do was to see the family got a few of the decent
things in life everyone else has. Not a lot of luxuries, just
what nowadays is the basics of a standard of living better
than it was in my father's day. A house, a second-hand
car, television, a washing machine so the wife doesn't have
to labour like her mother did, a fridge, perhaps two weeks
holiday in Spain where the sun is. These aren't things much
different from what most people have. You've worked for
them, got them gradually one by one: we don't have
nothing on HP. You think to yourself 'Well I've earned
them by my own hard work, I'm entitled to them as much
as someone who makes his living on the stock exchange
selling shares.'

And you hope in their time your kids'll grow up to do
that little bit better than you've done, because they have
the chance of more of an education. So you go on like
that. When the strike comes you support it, because you
think it's justified. It's for a good reason, and all your
mates are in it, and you stand by your mates. It wasn't
for a greedy reason, the strike: wanting more money or
something of that sort, it wasn't nothing like that. Or to
take over power from the Government. Though God
knows we couldn't have made a worse mess of it than
they've done in the last few years, eh? It wasn't for any of
those things. It was purely and simply about a man's right
to work, not to be thrown out on his ear from his life's
work because it was supposed to be for the good of the
country, or so he was told. What good it is for the country
to put millions of people out of work without the chance
of them ever getting a job again though is something I
can't follow and never will be able to. A man has a right
to his work.

But you didn't hear anything about that from Mrs

Thatcher* and her Tories. According to her, the only people who had the right to work were those who wanted to go in and break the strike. And it was like they were all on the same side: the press, the television, the Coal Board, the Government weren't they? You felt everybody was against you, everybody was saying you ought to accept redundancy and sit on your backside, or transfer, because you weren't any use to anybody anymore where you were. And then the day came when she said me and my mates were the enemy within. Within our own society, that it was our work that had created. Like somebody spitting in your face, eh? In all my lifetime, those words made more impression on me than anything anyone else's ever said.

I vote Labour like everyone does mostly in this part of the world. But I don't consider myself a political person, not really. So does that give right to a person like her in another party to insult me, tell me I'm not a true Englishman? If I'm her enemy then, what I say is I'm proud to be. I know who're the decent people of this country. I'm on their side, not on the side of her lot who think the country and its wealth all belongs to them. The enemy within, eh? And I thought I was just one of your ordinary people like.

– The strike started when the Coal Board said they were closing down Cortonwood Colliery in Yorkshire. I believe they'd told them not so long before they were going to be all right, their jobs were safe. Then they made the announcement of the closure. Yorkshire stopped more or less straight away, and each area was asked to vote whether to support them or not. Here and all over the north-east, we were pretty solid. At Red Hill we had the meeting, I went, and on the vote we were almost a hundred per cent for striking. And from then on all through the strike we had a meeting every Sunday in the Welfare Hall in the

---

* The Rt Hon Margaret Thatcher, MP: at the time Prime Minister and Leader of the Conservative Party.

village, where anyone who wanted could come along and put their point of view. One or two did say they thought we were never going to win, and one or two that we ought to have a national ballot. But there was never no animosity about it, nothing like fighting or even bad temper even. People listened to other people's points of view and if it was demanded there was a vote about something. There was only the odd one now and again voted for ending the strike, there was never bad feeling. Those who did vote against the majority, they didn't in any way suffer for it: and even though they didn't agree with it they always went along with what the majority wanted.

But you know, those Nottingham men weren't going to strike, right from the beginning they weren't. Some did, a few: but now you look back at it we must have been potty to think most ever would. They're among some of the highest-paid miners in the country. They've got big seams that thick, they get out a big lot of coal and they earn themselves a big lot of money. More than twice what most of us do round here or in Yorkshire. There was no way the majority of them were going to vote themselves out of that. And that suited the Coal Board and the Government very well.

As everyone will tell you, you can see it now very clearly what was going on eh, as plain as the nose on your face. The Government wanted to break the Union. That was it, at bottom that was what it was fundamentally all about, to break the power of the strongest union in the country, the National Union of Mineworkers.

Geoff's better on all this than I am. He'll explain it to you more clearly if you want to know the details. For me like I said, I was going along with my mates. I didn't like being on strike, I'd never say that to you: I'd sooner be at work. But I could see it was very important, if we didn't take a stand we wouldn't have any work left for us all to go to.

The first few weeks or so, I did, I used to sit here looking at these walls and not knowing what to do. I'd go out for a walk, or go down the Welfare Hall and see some of the lads and talk. We were all thinking at the beginning it couldn't go on indefinitely, it'd bound to be settled in a few weeks. It didn't dawn on us you know – at least it didn't dawn on me – that the Government had been preparing for it for a very long time and they were going to sit tight and see it out. We kept seeing on the television about the fighting that was going on outside pits. We didn't properly understand it. You got the impression if you didn't know any better that it was happening all day long outside every pit in the country. But it wasn't: it didn't happen here, not at Red Hill at all till towards the very end.

A lot of others like me felt we weren't really doing enough. It seemed to be a sort of nothing-happening time for a long time: like I say, it was only gradually we came to see it was going to go on and go on. Then we heard one day there was going to be a big rally down in Nottingham-shire, at Mansfield I think it was in about the middle of June. A lot of us decided we'd go and show solidarity. And I can honestly say to you that although it was a big demonstration, it was a good-humoured one, a cheerful one: it definitely was at the beginning. There was one or two, you always get them eh, it doesn't matter if it's a football crowd or what, they've had a drink and they start a bit of needling. So yes there were a few like that. And there were a lot of police there and most of them from what I've heard were fairly placid like. But they've got their hot-headed ones too like anyone else. And they come together with some of the same sort among ours. What happened next is obvious, well there was a bit of a scrap, but nothing very serious at all.

I'd gone along myself out of interest more than anything. We have big rallies up here now and again, it was some-thing to do to go and look at someone else's. There was a group of us standing together at the side of a road leading towards the field where the main part of the rally was going to be, and then all of a sudden a big white police transit van pulled up by the side of us. About ten or twelve coppers jumped out, grabbed the nearest men to them, and shoved them in the back of the van. I mean they hadn't done anything at all, but they was pushed in and the van roared off with them out of sight. I stood there with my mouth open, I couldn't believe what I'd just seen. And then I don't know if it was a minute later or five minutes later or what: but before we could turn round another police van pulled up, and this time it was the turn of me and about eight others. They jumped out, grabbed us, pushed us into the van, slammed the door and locked it, and whizzed us off. I read somewhere later they called them 'snatch squads', well that's just what they were. When we got to the police station we were pushed out of the van and up to that point nobody'd said anything to us, not a word. And then we were all taken into a room and told we were going to be charged.

None of us could make out what was going on at all. There was a lot of shouting and pushing about of people, but it wasn't violent. But you couldn't get anyone to tell you what was happening. It seemed like one of those crazy scenes in a film. But the long and short of it was we was all kept in custody for two days, then brought up in front of a magistrate who said we could be let out on bail on condition we stayed in our own homes. Not just stay out of Nottinghamshire, but stay up here in Durham in our own homes. When I got back the wife was going potty: she didn't know if I'd had an accident or what. One of the coppers had told me our families'd be informed, but none of them was. I'd never been in a police station before in my life except to make an inquiry. It gave me a completely different picture, not one that was a very nice one at all.

What I was charged with, I didn't realise it at the time but it was really something very serious. Riotous assembly. I didn't twig at first how serious it was, because I hadn't done anything. I didn't know in those days the police made up things, that they stood up in court and swore lies were true. Time went on at home and none of us heard anything:

it was only gradually like that we began to find out what it was we were facing. To put it bluntly it was a chance of long imprisonment. When I heard it first time I didn't believe it: but I went and looked it up in reference books in the library. I found out it was true, it could carry a sentence of prison for up to your whole life.

I kept hoping that the charge would come up and be dismissed and over with, because to tell you the truth I was getting into a bad state mentally about it. Maureen kept saying I shouldn't worry, nothing could happen because I hadn't done anything, I wasn't the person they thought I was. But I couldn't sleep, I was getting to dream horrible dreams and all the time building up in my mind what might be going to happen. I can understand how people can get to the state when they commit suicide. We had no money coming in except for the Social Security, which was £40-odd for the five of us. The wife's parents and my parents helped us out, they were both wonderful to us, if it hadn't been for them I don't know we'd have got through. We're still paying them back though, and I don't mind telling you it's going to take a long time.

So then all that waiting, I was sitting looking at the walls again at home, worrying about this charge hanging over me, thinking I'd better be careful not to do anything that would sound like an infringement of bail conditions. I used to walk along to the Welfare Hall and hope there was no one from Nottinghamshire in the village who might see me, because I wasn't strictly keeping to the terms of staying in my home see. But I'd have gone round the twist if I hadn't gone out at all. I passed my time during the day at first playing endless games of snooker, then I got to feeling that I didn't want to go and waste all my days like that, so I helped out in the kitchen where they were giving out hot meals to the lads. I was washing up dishes in the back. I couldn't go on the picket line down here at the pit. If they picked me up they'd say I was breaking my bail, so washing up dishes was as much as I could do.

That charge was hanging over me just over a total of

twelve months. Then we went to Nottingham for the trial, and we were all tried in batches. I wasn't in the first lot, but they were acquitted by the jury because of the suspect police evidence. I was in a later batch – who after all that, they didn't proceed with because they'd failed with the first lot. So in the end it all came to nothing. All that worry, all that wondering, all those times I'd felt sick to my stomach, everything Maureen had gone through and the kids – and it all came down to them dropping the charge. But the police weren't doing us any favours, they hadn't dropped the charge out of the kindness of their hearts. It was only because the jury didn't believe the evidence they gave about those who'd been put in the dock first. It gives you a sour feeling eh? My first experience of the police force and the British legal system. Well – another beer?

The good old solid Union man
Geoff Danson

Across the yard and round the back of the high building of the pithead baths, an old wooden hut huddled up against the wall. Not much more than a garden shed. Inside it was cramped: a table, two chairs, a filing cabinet and some bookshelves piled with files and pamphlets and documents. A ceiling strip light for illumination. On the desk a telephone, empty tea mugs, overflowing ashtrays, forms: the air acrid with cigarette smoke. The Union office. The man at the desk was big and silver-haired, his voice gravelly and slow.

– Oh aye I can tell it you off the top of my head. In 1981 Arthur Scargill was President of the NUM with the biggest members' vote there'd ever been in the history of the Union. In March '83 Thatcher appointed her elderly American gentleman MacGregor to be Chairman of the Coal Board. In June she and Tories won the election again with a landslide, and in September MacGregor came to the Board and started his work. Six months later, this'd be March 1984, the NCB announced at short notice they were going to close Cortonwood Colliery in Yorkshire, and as a result of that, there was a Yorkshire area strike which the Executive of the NUM declared official.

In this area we went on strike to support Yorkshire the following week, and secondary picketing – or at least that's what the Coal Board called it – started at some factories in the area which made machinery for the mines. The pits themselves were pretty solidly out till Christmas: a few went back then but not many. It wasn't till February 1985 that the return to work seriously began, and then by the end of that month fifty per cent of the workforce was back. The strike was called off, and there was the official return to work on Tuesday 5 March.

So that's about the history, the chronological list of events like. And up till that time there'd been no suggestion at all that Red Hill might be closed. It wasn't until this May the NCB let it be known they were thinking of it. We've put the case against it, and we've asked for it to be submitted to the Board's review procedure before any final decision is taken. We're now waiting for that now. I'm not very hopeful of the outcome myself because I've no faith at all in the Board. But we'll see. Sorry Joe, can you come back in a bit, d'you mind?

Me? I've been working in this pit for thirty-three years. I started in the yard out there, two days after my fifteenth birthday, humping bits of wood about. My father was a miner here before me, and I've a younger brother here who's been in the pit thirty years. Yes I once considered an alternative: when I'd been a year here I thought I might fancy going to sea on one of them coal barges running up and down the coast. I don't know where I might have ended up if I had, but I still look back and wish I'd had perhaps a year or so of it for the experience. But my mother didn't want it so I never got to do it. I seem to remember she had the idea I should work a few years in the pit to get a bit of money before trying something else. But at the finish I stayed where I was, and I've been a working miner ever since.

At the moment I'm a man in a little office taking telephone calls, answering queries from the fellers who keep coming in through that door and interrupting us, writing letters, making up rotas and lists, keeping accounts, and all this other paraphernalia. But I'm not really a pen and ink man, I'm a working miner. For most of the last few years I've been a power loader, which is a worker on the coalface. That's where my heart is. Some people might say I was well off here with a nice clean job. But I think it's easier mentally working down the pit. In this job my time isn't my own when I go home: I'm all the time thinking in my head what's going to come up tomorrow. I've got much more thinking here than I've ever done in my life before and try to be tolerant to all points of view. I'm not my own man, I'm the men's representative. So I've not got to let it affect me whether they were solid with the Union all through the strike, or whether some of them have been transferred here because in the strike they scabbed at other pits. I'm also aware there are a few here who scabbed here. But I've got to swallow my feelings and remember they're all in the Union and it's my job to represent every single member.

My wife says she's noticed a big change in me since I started to work here in the office. She says it's a change for the better, it's made me listen to people more than I used to: I'm easier to live with and not so argumentative she says. My son and daughter, they say the same thing: so I can't have been all that good at listening can I, in the past, for them all to say that?

Oh yes there've been a big lot of changes in the pit in my time, yes a hell of a lot. I'd say the main one is the amount of mechanisation there is now underground. I'm a power loader, which is someone who operates the machine that rips out the coal, but I can still remember the time when men actually hacked it out with picks and drills. They were called colliers and they were regarded as the *crème de la crème*. You counted yourself privileged to be working with one of them if you were a youngster. It was your job to shovel back the coal that he hacked out. You put it in a tub, which was a container like a small railway trolley: and then it was hauled back from the coalface into the main road, and from there it went on along to the pit bottom and up to the surface. In those days, the tubs were perhaps big enough to carry two or three hundredweight of coal, and all the haulage of them was by ropes. Now it's mechanical conveyor belts, big trucks that take tons of coal, and all the haulage is by diesels. The roads you work in nowadays are higher too. Nowadays nearly everyone works standing up, but when I first come in the pit you were lucky if you could do that. The tunnels were only half as high then as they are today, and now they're supported with steel girders and lined with corrugated sheeting, and all things like that. And it's all much cleaner and lighter than it used to be. So in pretty well everything there's been an enormous big improvement in the working conditions.

But I don't think people who haven't been down a mine really still realise though how primitive pits are in many ways. For a start you'll get people who're surprised when you tell them there are no toilets down there or anything of that sort. When you want to do whatever it is you want to do, you either do it where you're standing or go off into one of the unused side roads. Then when it comes to break time for you to have your meal, there's the old saying 'Look before you sit, don't sit where someone shit.' And of course there's no canteens or washing facilities or things of that sort. So like I say we're very primitive in that respect. Old-fashioned is another word. Then there's the anti-social hours. I've never been able to work out why some shifts start at four in the morning. When you ask, all people can tell you is it's always been like that. I suppose there must be a reason for it but I couldn't tell you what it was.

And so what I'm going to say now will maybe surprise you. It's that in my opinion the working atmosphere you get down a pit, in spite of what I've been talking about is absolutely unique in industry. The comradeship and friendship of it is very special. I believe there's a word for it isn't there, camaraderie? That's what there is among you and your mates when you're a miner. When you're riding in that cage and you're all being dropped like a bloody stone to the bottom of that shaft every day of your working life, you're always aware you're all mates together. It might sound a strange thing to say to some people, but to me it's still a thrill, there's something very exciting about it I can't properly explain. You ask any miner and I'd bet he'll tell you the same. The feeling you all work together and depend on one another, you all run the same risks: it's something of that. Yes William it's all right, come in, what can I do for you?

– The day shift's gone, tonight we can have an hour not interrupted if you like, OK?

You hear a lot about the community feeling, and it's very true. It's not just down the pit that you're dependent on your mates, it's everywhere. You're all in the same job, you're all in the same place and you all depend upon one another. That's what's been built up over generations and that's what this Government's trying to break down. It does, it causes great bitterness.

As to why they should do it, well different people have got different ideas. I'd say it was my opinion when that woman talks of a return to Victorian values, what she's got in her mind is a return to the sort of society where there was two levels – the masters and the servants. At the top you had a few people who were the employers and the people who made a lot of money, and then you had the lower level of person whose labour they used to make their big profits. What they want to do is get back to those times, if they're going to be honest about it.

It wasn't all that long time ago you know, only about eight years or so, they were recruiting men in a big drive for labour in a lot of the pits round here: and in particular for this one. 'Come into the Top League' they said on the posters, I can remember them now. The Board was saying there were secure jobs here for life, and the future was very bright. I won't say they were deliberately lying, I don't like to accuse anyone of that. But they were misleading people and playing about with people's lives. They may well have found out they were mistaken – though I wouldn't personally accept that, I think there's been a lot of mismanagement and there's still a lot of good coal to be mined. But they shouldn't at one time have told a man to come to Red Hill, then only a few years later told him he wasn't wanted any more when they'd been promising him a future like they did. That's criminal.

And the strike – well what happened during that and what happened after it, I could go on for a year about it. So could any person who was involved in it, not only Geoff

Danson the good old solid Union man. It was the worst experience of my life was that, and I'd say of most men's lives in this area. Margaret Thatcher and the Coal Board set out to crush the National Union of Miners, that was the long and short of it. She hasn't succeeded yet, but it's in the balance. I think there's a lot of people thought they wanted that too, because the power of the unions in general was too strong. But it'll be a bad day for the working man of this country if she succeeds in what she's trying to do.

The NUM's always been the strongest and most united union in the land, you know, but at the strike we were divided. The Government waited until they were ready to have a confrontation, and then they sprung the closure of Cortonwood. Right in the heart of a big mining area, and not far from the Union's headquarters. I think they chose that place deliberately. And I think they chose the ground they were going to fight on, and left Arthur Scargill no choice but to strike. They took careful soundings before the thing started, and they knew the Union was going to be divided because the strike wasn't about money. The Coal Board knew that Nottingham wouldn't support us. So they built up the coal stocks, and they formed a police force on a national basis: one that could be mobilised and sent here there or wherever they were needed to stop the picketing. It enabled them, when they were ready, to use brute force to get men in through the picket lines. It was all very clever: and it put Nottingham to thinking we were trying to stop them earning their good money. But I think Nottingham'll live to regret it. They'll be picked off later after they've dealt with us. Privatisation of the mines is what the Tories are after, and unless there's an awakening to that among the whole mining community, we're going to find ourselves back in the old world of lockouts and poverty and all the rest of it.

Thatcher brought in her man MacGregor, a man known to be all his life totally against unions, known all his life to have devoted himself to the breaking of unions in the USA. And she couldn't have got a better man to carry out what she wanted done. He was exactly right for her. He weeded out from the Coal Board any of the old pit men who were sympathetic to the miners, and only kept those who were prepared to stay there and behave in the way he told them to.

There had to be a strike, there can't be question of that. In view of Cortonwood the Union would have been made to look like impotent windbags if it'd backed down. All the talk about a ballot, well that was just a smokescreen the Government put up. I think anyway if it'd all been properly explained there'd have been the majority for strike action. The Coal Board was happy to let it drag on and show the country that the miners were divided. To my mind it was a mortal blow not just to the NUM, but to the whole of the trades union movement, and from now on there'll be more and more Government taking on of all the unions.

We have this mean and terrible Government, and the whole country's being put into the situation where there are going to be only two sorts of people: the working-class people and the middle-class people, and the Government will have set them completely against each other. Class versus class: and I'm sorry to say it's getting to be north against south too. I don't think people in the southern part of England really have much idea of the suffering of unemployment up here. They certainly didn't understand the strike. On the television all the concentration was on the battles on the picket lines, the police versus the miners, the miners versus the scabs. I mean as far as working miners are concerned, some of them are not all honey and spice, everyone knows that. But what I'm saying is all the reporting was about confrontation, no one ever tried to explain what case the miners really had. We're not extremists, we want work and decent pay for our work and a decent standard of living. What we don't want is to be cast as though we were some kind of unimportant labour force to be used or not according to when it suited the bosses.

I think most people believe like I do, that you should

earn money rather than make it: earn it by your own work, not make money by gambling on the stock exchange with other people's money. We believe people should have equal opportunities, there ought to be decent education for everyone, a good standard of health care, a good standard of life all round generally. But this Government doesn't believe any of that. It talks about individual enterprise, but to me that's just another expression for taking advantage of others.

You know if you take into account the social consequences, the cost of redundancy money and then paying out the dole and Social Security to families for years – if you do all that, what it costs to close a mine could keep it open for a further ten years. It's not just me saying this and making up figures: this is what people have worked out for us, researchers in the Union. What sort of a country is it we live in, when everything's worked out on the basis of whether the coal that comes out of the ground is sold at an economic price? There's much more to it than that. The coal goes to the electricity generating stations mostly, and they produce the electricity for industry and for people's homes. And they produce it with coal at a much cheaper price than they ever could do with atomic energy. They'll tell you how cheap it is to produce a given unit of electricity by nuclear energy. But if you count into that the millions of pounds cost they've had in building the atomic power stations, the two figures aren't even comparable. There should have been the same amount of investment in the coal mines, because that would have been invested in people's lives.

You can't dig out the nation's mineral wealth from the ground and its mental wealth from inside people. But that's what this Government seems to be wanting to do: perhaps not exactly dig it out but cover it over as though it didn't have any value.

But as a Union man, you know, I have to say this is how the Tories came to power, this is what they said they would do. At the time of the last Labour government they said if they got back in, they'd bring in legislation to reduce the power of the trades unions. And they've certainly done it all right. It's my opinion, and I think of a large part of the working class of this country, certainly the four million or so that's unemployed, they've gone so far now in breaking the power of the unions they've put the country back into the 1930s.

I think people were stupid to fall for it when the Tories said they were going to achieve an economic miracle by reordering society. But they have reordered it and they're going on reordering it: not with an economic miracle for everyone but with a few at the top and a lot at the bottom. I think it'll be many years before we get over the damage that's been done. I don't greatly care whether the Labour Party is right, left or centre – that doesn't seem as important to me as the fact it was built up on union power, and it was built up for the good of all working people. Nobody gave the workers of this country what they have today. They had to take it: they had to bargain and they could get what they wanted because of the power being organised had brought them.

But the ruling class hangs on as long as it can to what it has, and it always will. It's now every day getting a bigger and bigger share of the country's wealth. And do people honestly think it's going to give it up, or more correctly give it back, out of the goodness of its heart?

No chance of a football life for me
Harry Hartley

'A scab is a two-legged animal with a corkscrew soul, a waterlogged brain, a combination backbone of jelly and glue. Where others have a heart, he carries a tumour of rotten principles. When a scab comes down the street, men turn their backs, the angels weep in Heaven, and the Devil shuts the gates of Hell to keep him out. No man has a right to scab so long as there is a pool of water to drown his carcass in, or a rope long enough to hang his body with.'

– It was Jack London that wrote that. We had it run off on a duplicator for us, we gave them out to our mates at other pits who were having more trouble with scabs than we did here at Red Hill. There wasn't no trouble here, we can hold our heads up and say we was solid almost to the end of the strike. Altogether it wasn't more than ten or a dozen right at the very end. And most of them were only 9 out of 10 mentally if you know what I mean. They didn't know what day it was, what they were doing, what was happening. What was worse they didn't know what would happen to them. I know one, I think his name's Norman something. He's only a lad, and he's daft as a brush. I don't understand the mentality of people like that. I'm an ordinary Union man myself, and scabbing is something I couldn't ever do. Letting down your mates that you worked all your life with, you don't do that sort of thing. If the majority says strike then we strike. We can argue the toss about it, we can listen to one point of view and another, but if the majority is for something then that's what the Union's about, doing what the majority decides.

A small man, forty-six, brown-eyed and smiling. He sat on the edge of the sofa in the sitting room of his small and plainly furnished bungalow, gently fondling the ears of a silky-haired spaniel that lay with its eyes closed, its head on his lap.

– When I was a lad still at school I had the chance to sign on for an apprentice with Middlesbrough Football Club. In those days they were one of the big teams in the north-east, First Division they were. I thought I was going to be in heaven for the rest of my life. There I was, one of ten children – the littlest one and the youngest one, and I was going to play for Middlesbrough Football Club. I think one of their scouts had picked me out at some schoolboy game. But it didn't happen. Whether I funked it or not when I got there, I don't properly remember. I know all my confidence seemed to go altogether, and no sooner was there that serious chance there than I didn't want to go on with it. I think I can't have done well in trials because my parents heard nothing more about it. That was the beginning and end of my career. Bang, no chance of a football life for me. Funny when you think about it, if I'd have gone on who'd I'd have been? Wilf Mannion the Second, eh? Things'd have been very different in my life wouldn't they?

I've had thirty-two years at Red Hill. I've enjoyed being a miner and in some respects I've had a good life but not in others. I wasn't no good at school and I couldn't get away early enough from it. All I was interested in was sport. I wasn't broken-hearted or things of that sort about the Middlesbrough business. I knew in my heart I hadn't got it in me to make the big time, not really. And anyway in those days you didn't get the money they do nowadays.

I left school on the Friday morning, had my medical at the pit on the Friday afternoon, and started work the following Monday. I was on the surface for a year where I had training for underground such as it was, then it was exactly on my sixteenth birthday I went down underground. There, first of all I was what they called a datal lad: that's someone employed by the day doing mostly odd-job work. The datal lad is the one who gets sent here there and everywhere along the different roads on the haulage to anywhere he's needed. He's the one that gets the lowest pay, and it's just like another sort of training period to get you used to working underground.

I did that for a time, then I went regular on the haulage, then on the loading belt. I think after that I was on maintenance and safety. You gradually get more responsible jobs and bigger jobs. Now I've got on to the top rate because I'm a power loader. It's working with big machinery, heavy stuff: it can be a bit dangerous so you've got to have your wits about you. I wouldn't say it was difficult work but it's good work and I like it. You get some sort of satisfaction out of it, to be actually cutting the coal.

From the pit bottom, the face I'm working on now is about a half-hour journey on one of them little trains. I wouldn't say we've got all that bad conditions, they'd done a lot of mechanisation and modernisation in the pit since I started, but on what you might call the hygiene side things aren't much better than they were twenty years ago. Some of the coal faces are as high as six foot: there are lower ones but the coal's difficult to work in them because the seams are thinner and they're gradually phasing them out. The main things better since the days when I started is that the ventilation's improved a lot, and there are hydraulic supports on the face along the roads. In the old days it all used to be timber supports. The old colliers used to say that timber was better because if a support was going to break you got a bit of warning, you could hear the wood starting to crack. But with a steel support it just snaps and that's it. But you don't get the accidents, the roof falls at the face and all the rest of it that you used to. The coal industry's safety record has improved out of all recognition. Accidents nowadays aren't so often at the face: when they happen they're usually on haulage, people getting injured through being careless.

I expect others'll say the same thing to you, that down the pit everyone gets on together. You work with all your mates, so it's good. There is one little thing creeping in now though since the strike, and that I'm not happy about. It's that they don't like you getting too much in a tight group with the same mates: they try and move you around, and break up your groups and form new ones. They do this regular now, it's something the management's adopted as deliberate policy. I think they were told after the strike not to let this happen, men being so firm together all the time. We've all talked about this a lot, and we do all think it's the Board's policy. And a thing that it does is it affects production: when you were all working like one man you were a more efficient working unit. That's something else they're not very keen on nowadays. If they've got your pit down for closure, which our suspicion is about Red Hill, they want to break up production and the unity of the men as well.

Before the strike, it was always said Red Hill was one of the friendliest pits there was in the whole of the north-east coalfields. There was a lot of the feeling of being all in it together with the management too. We had a good man as manager most of the time I've been there, and everyone were proud of the relationship. But he went, and then since the strike there's been a different atmosphere altogether. No one knows what's going to happen, everyone's uncertain and unhappy over things, and the management's having a lot of its power taken away from it. It's not the pit it was, nothing like. The sort of thing you get now is that if there was going to be a Union meeting about something and we thought there'd be a lot there, we'd ask the manager if we could have the use of a certain room in the offices. He never turned us down, he'd always say it was OK and go ahead. But now suddenly the Board's told him he's got to ask them first. And last week, the first time he asked them they've turned us down.

And the big thing makes everyone unhappy is they were saying ten years ago there was enough coal in Red Hill to last nearly a hundred years. And now what're they saying? That it's a big loss-maker, it's uneconomic and we're losing money hand over fist. It's the sort of thing I couldn't ever have imagined, not if I'd been talking to you five years ago, I would never have imagined anything of that sort.

What they've done is put in to the Coal Board a whole lot of business men, managers, accountants – and all of them MacGregor's men. He tells them to produce different figures to the ones they put out before: he'll set them on to a pit and before you can turn round they've brought out figures which show you your pit is a loss-maker. Distrust, suspicion, looking over the shoulder: these are the features now, it's a nasty atmosphere I'll tell you that straight out.

– Tonight the strike? OK yes. Well I don't think the Union had any choice about the strike, they had to take the action they did. I'm not a great believer in Arthur Scargill as a matter of fact, I think he let himself be outmanoeuvred. The Coal Board knew better than he did what was going on. Their stocks were high, they knew they could recruit non-Union drivers to move coal, they knew they'd got the whole summer ahead of them. They worked out their plans and their strategy, and it included mobile police to move around wherever they wanted them. I've heard it said some of the police weren't police, they were army men, soldiers. I think that's very likely from the descriptions I've heard how they marched in certain places. Those who were there say they didn't march like policemen, they marched like soldiers. But there's a lot of rumours, you can't tell whether they're true or not: but that particular one is a very common one.

About Scargill, well you have to hand it to the man that he was honest, and his principles were right. From the very start he said there was a hit list for pits: that the Coal Board were going to close down a lot more and put a lot more men out of work than they were letting on about. He didn't say one thing to his members and another to the bosses: he said we had to resist closures, and if we didn't do it successfully in a few years' time we'd find the industry had been ruined and most of its men would be unemployed.

He didn't say there should be no closures at all: what he did say was things could be done, and should be done, in a slower fashion with more discussion. He said other factors besides the immediate cost per ton of getting coal out of the ground should be taken into account, and management and Union should work together, take steps to consider social consequences as well as just accountants' figures about particular pits. There's some pits kept working that haven't produced any coal for a very long time: and they're kept going because they're needed for linking up with other underground systems, or ventilation, or taking down machinery, to approach faces other ways, things of that sort. So if you're going to talk about pits being uneconomic in terms of how much it costs them to produce a ton of coal, well ones like them are not producing any coal at all. But they're kept open.

I think Scargill was wrong in some of his methods. He'd have done better to have put over his case and then called for a national ballot. He'd probably have got his majority. There was a feeling in the summer that most of his members would go along with him even if some areas didn't. It was a pity it turned out like it did, and it's easy to look back now and say he ought to have done this or that. That Thatcher woman was very clever, much cleverer and more devious than he was. I don't think he really paid sufficient attention to how clever she was, he underestimated her. And that's one thing you couldn't say the other way round, that she underestimated him. He let her push him into the strike by the deliberate provocation of closing Cortonwood – right on his doorstep, almost as though she was baiting him by choosing that one. And he fell for it. But until the day somebody can prove Arthur Scargill said something that wasn't right, and behaved in a deceitful way, until that day the man'll have my respect. You don't ever have to ask yourself whose side is he on, you know he's one hundred per cent for the miners.

I'd still go through it all again, the strike: I wouldn't like to, but I would if I had to. It wasn't just a strike for more

money, it wasn't a greedy or a selfish strike, it was a strike
about principles. There's nothing to be ashamed of in
trying to preserve your way of life, especially when you're
not even asking to do it at the expense of other people.
We've got a history and a tradition in the mines, and that's
something very valuable. To try and smash that, like the
Government's doing, well that seems to me to be a very
wicked thing to do.

Some people have said it wasn't so much a strike, it was
a protest. The Government needed telling they couldn't
just treat people as though they were slaves, have them in
work one day and chuck them out the next, just for the
sake of their own political ideas about how to run an
economy. For a man who's worked hard all his life to be
told what she was saying – that he was expendable, he
couldn't be afforded, it was for the good of the country –
that was a terrible thing to say. I don't see wrong in
protesting about that. I'd like to say to Mrs Thatcher what
I feel, that we can't as a country afford her. The difference
is that when she gets out of a job, as she will do one day,
she'll live in a very nice house and with a very nice pension
thank you very much. For the rest of her life she'll not be
living like millions of the likes of us. I don't suppose though
she ever loses any sleep about it. And she'll certainly not
ever come up here and start distributing some of her
private cash to people who're having a hard time for the
rest of their lives because of her.

– If I hadn't been a miner I think what I'd most liked to
have been was a gamekeeper, you know led an outdoor
life. I've never had the brains to be a person who works
in an office, you need an education for that. I'm just a
hard worker. I don't mean they don't work hard in offices,
but me and my sort of person have been brought up to
think when you talk about hard work you mean physical
labour. I don't read books very much, that's not something
I enjoy. I suppose that goes back to your education too.
So when it comes to like now when I have to think of the

future, it's not a thing that comes easy to me. I haven't got enough money to retire, and if I took redundancy the payment I got wouldn't let me sit down and take a rest for a few years. I'd straight away have to start thinking what was to come next. The wife and I are separated and have been for a good while. She's got the children and I've them to provide for as well as her. And when you get to my age you can feel you're getting older, you know physical things are going to happen to you that make you less of a worker. Deterioration, illnesses, accidents, those are all prospects which become more likely. I was thinking the other night about what I'd been saying to you about once perhaps being a footballer. I remembered my dad told me he didn't think it was a very good idea because there was no future in football. But he'd never have said to me there was no future in being a miner, that's something he wouldn't have said. But I have to say that to my son: I have to tell him whatever he does he can't think there's a future for him in the mines. There isn't. No matter what the Coal Board says, however much they dangle promises in front of people's eyes about some new superpits they're going to open over the next few years.

It's very very quiet now down the pit
Norman Lane

Slightly built and with long curly hair down almost to his shoulders, he poked nervously at the fire in the front room of a cold unfurnished council house, five miles from the village, on the far edge of a poorly lit housing estate. He sat on a packing case, his voice thin and tense, his eyes and hands ill-at-ease.

– I didn't want to talk, I didn't want to meet you really. That tape recorder thing, I don't like tape recorders. My Uncle John said I should talk to you, that's all why I'm talking to you. He said he didn't agree with me but I've a right to my point of view. He said everyone has a right to their point of view, I ought to put mine. Only don't give my real name or address. I've been in this house three weeks tomorrow, and I don't want people to know where I am. It's got nothing to do with them anyway. I don't expect there'd be any trouble now, but it's best to be on the safe side. In a few months things will have settled down. And anyway then I shan't be at Red Hill any longer. They've told me I can soon have a transfer, then things'll be better. But at the moment I don't want things about me being in a book or anything like that.

I'm twenty-five and I started at Red Hill pit five years ago. I'd had a packing job in a factory at Peterlee, but it closed down and then I was unemployed. I'd come to Red Hill because I'd read those adverts they'd had in the papers saying it was one of their new pits and there was going to be secure jobs there for ten years. I hadn't really intended working in the mines, I didn't fancy it, but there wasn't anything else going. The wife and I'd not been long married and the baby was on the way, so that was a factor. I thought well if I stick it it's a job for life. My brothers are both in the army, they're older than me and they seem to quite like it: but they often have a long time away from home, so that didn't appeal to me. I thought I'll have a few years at the pit, save up some money, and then I'll go on to something else. Unemployment wasn't as bad five years ago as it is now, but when my Uncle John told me there was a chance of getting into Red Hill I thought it'd be for the best. I've never liked it much there though, the people aren't very friendly. If you don't live in the village you're not really one of them you see, they don't take to you. My wife was a Red Hill girl herself, but she said she was glad to get away from there, there was such a lot of gossip and backbiting and that.

I started at twenty, thereabouts. Like everyone else they put me on the bank, that's on the surface for a few months to begin with, then I went underground for a datal lad. I was mostly on the conveyor belts, pushing a button, that was all there was to it. I did that for about three year, as far as hard work was concerned it was about the easiest job I've ever had in my life. The only thing with it was that where I was working was where one of the engines was, for one of the extractor fans: it was noisy and windy and it got very very cold sometimes too. I suppose it was a bit boring but I've never been much for talking and skylarking about with other people on the job so I didn't mind that. So long as I was left alone and being well paid for it, I was happy.

The Union wasn't something I had much to do with. Because we didn't live in the village but on the outskirts of Peterlee, on the other side of the estate here, I think they looked at it I was an outsider. I could have gone to Union meetings if I'd wanted to, but I've never seen much point to it. When I get my transfer, if I get to Waddell Moor I've heard there's very few there keen on the Union, so it'll make things better for me, I won't be one on my own so much. It's about ten miles away from here, and I'll be able to go because they have buses which they put on for the start of the different shifts. The main thing about it for me will be over half the men working there went back during the strike before Christmas, so there won't be many that can say anything to me.

I only went back to work at Red Hill two weeks before the strike finished. I don't see what I did was all that terrible, I don't see I should be victimised for it like I am. The week after I went back there was twenty men at Red Hill back at work altogether, and some of those don't get anything like the hard time now that I do. I know who they were, most of them were on the coach with me in the morning when we were being bussed in to the pit by the Board. They collected us from a different place each day. You had to phone up the night before and then they'd tell you where to be at what time in the morning the following day. It was a different place each time, because if anyone had found out where it was then very likely they'd have sent people there and there would have been trouble. It was very nasty being bussed in past the pickets: stones was thrown, there was shouting and all the rest of it, men banging their fists on the sides, trying to break the windows of the bus with shovel handles. They gave us those woollen hats to wear, balaclavas they call them, so we wouldn't be identified. But some of the pickets got our names and had them up on a board. I think some of the men working in the pit on safety cover got the names, they found them out from the wages office. Someone did tip the pickets off, there's no argument about that and it wasn't very nice.

– I don't want no one to hear these tapes, I wouldn't say things if I thought others was going to listen to them. I've talked to my uncle and he says I imagine things, you're nothing to do with the Union. But when you're living the life I'm living now, all sorts of ideas come into your mind. One idea I had was you might give the Union the tape, and they'd somehow use it against me. My uncle said I was daft. But I wouldn't talk to you if I thought there'd be any chance of anything of that sort.

I didn't think last week when we were talking I'd still be at Red Hill a week later, because I thought the Board would have moved me like they promised they would. I don't reckon they've been fair with me. No one from the Board has given me so much as a thank you for being one of the first to go back to work. I was one of the ones who was prepared to be amongst the first, and they used me and a few others to show the rest that they could get men into the pit. I think they owe me something for that, they shouldn't just leave me dangling in the air, they ought to give me my transfer like they said. The Coal Board was happy enough to stick us on buses as an example to others, but then what?

I don't like it at Red Hill, it's not a good atmosphere working there at all. I wouldn't say I was frightened, because they've all been told now the strike's over, if say a man raises his fists to another man, or anything of that sort, the man who does it'll get the sack on the spot. But the sort of thing that happens is you get in the cage to go down the shaft with the others, and they've all been talking and laughing. Then when you appear and get in, everyone goes silent. Then one or two at the back'll start making a hissing noise, very softly 'sssss-sssss' like that. It makes you feel scared. Or you'll hear someone start saying in a low voice 'Scab scab, scab scab', then someone else then someone else. And when you go past someone in the baths at the pit head, they shout out from behind you to someone further along 'Eh up Eric's coming.' If you turn round to try and see who's doing it, then nobody's looking at you are they: they don't do it to your face, only behind you round your back. Well, an Eric's from that thing used to be on television about Geordie builders: they called the Germans Erics. What was it called, *Auf Wiedersehen, Pet*.

I'm fed up to my back teeth with it, if they don't send me to Waddell Moor before long I shall get out. You see one of the problems now is that there's only two of us left at Red Hill who went back to work before the end of the strike. The others have all either transferred or taken redundancy and left, there's only me and this other bloke there now. I don't know his name, and we're not on the same shift: I think they've put him on maintenance. He might be having it easier. I've got to be on day shift all the time. I've asked if I could be on a different shift, but they said no for my own safety. I don't understand properly what they mean, I think they mean they've got to keep me working somewhere where someone can keep an eye on me all the time.

The under manager says that there's nothing for me to worry about, everyone knows there's to be no victimisation or they'll be sacked. He said I was to tell him if I had any trouble from anybody, he'd see the man was reprimanded. But in a way that's like being back at school and telling tales to the teacher. He's put me to work on my own down a short road off the pit bottom, I'm working a pump. There's no one within fifty feet of me, and it's a well-lit part, I'm not in any danger of anyone catching me when no one's looking. But I have a whole eight-hour shift on my own, no one to talk to at all. That sort of thing gets you down after a bit. All I do's just check that the pump's working properly and keep an eye on it. Sometimes there's hardly a sound. It's not noisy, not like the job I had before: it's very very quiet now down the pit.

– You see that's it, nobody's ever asked me why I went back. I didn't do it out of bloody-mindedness, nothing of that sort. In fact I didn't want to go back, I'd have stopped out if I could. But things at home you see, they were very very bad. The wife didn't seem to know what it was she wanted. One day she was telling me I should stand by my mates and stay out on strike with them no matter how long, then the next day she'd turn round and be telling me I was a lazy layabout and I ought to get back to work, I was having no thought for her or the kiddie. I think probably it was her mother who was at the bottom of it all. She lived over the other side of the other council estate we were on then, Eileen used to go over and see her a lot. When she come back she was always in a filthy temper, I think her mother geed her up. Rows weren't nothing new to us, we had rows as a normal thing like you do in any marriage: and all right I might have given her one now and again, but no worse than any other husband. Only as the strike went on and on, we had much more rowing: all the time, and everything got pretty bad.

The main thing that finished it was the washing machine. Eileen came out of the kitchen one day and she was shouting and swearing that the bloody thing had broken down again, she just couldn't put up with anything any longer. She went and phoned the electricity people and they sent someone round to look at it, and he said it was going to cost £36 to put it right. We hadn't got that sort of money because of being on strike so long. We'd got an electric bill that we hadn't paid anyway, and the electricity was going to be cut off as well. So there was going to be nothing else for it but that we'd have to do without the washing machine. So from then on Eileen used to put all the clothes in the pram and wheel it round to her mother's twice a week, and do the washing there. It wasn't too bad in the summer except when it was raining, but into October and November you can see her point of view that she'd had enough.

In the end came the time one day when she came back from her mother's and she said she'd really had enough then, she wasn't taking it any more. She went upstairs and packed her suitcase for herself and one for Mandy, then she went off saying she'd come back tomorrow at dinner time for the rest. She knew I'd have my meal down the Welfare Hall, and when I come home next day after that I found she'd done what she said, been back and gone off again, and we've been split up ever since. She's got half the things we had, half the furniture and the rest of it, and I've got the other half still unpacked which is why it looks a bit bare. I think she was unreasonable about it all through. We got food parcels when they made the distributions at the Hall: we got meals and my mam gave us things. But she and Eileen haven't ever hit it off between them. Eileen would take money from her mam but she wouldn't take nothing at all from mine, not even to buy something for me or our kiddie.

When it got right towards the end of the strike, I had a think. I'd had a miserable Christmas on my own because my parents had gone to see one of my brothers' families up in Scotland for Christmas. So I thought if I went back to work, perhaps I could start to get myself sorted out and see if Eileen would come back. Everybody knew the strike was coming to an end. I only jumped the gun a bit, that's all. But the way they treat you in the pit, you might be a bloody leper or something. I don't think it's fair they don't take into account what sort of a difficult time different people were having. It's changed my feelings towards the Union. They're always on about how you should stand by your mates, but they're not standing by me, they treat me as though I wasn't a proper human person.

A few weeks after the strike finished, Eileen came back for a few days. But it wasn't the same, I think it was less than a week before she went again, off back home to her mam. She said it'd never work for us. I don't miss her but I miss the kiddie. I've made a mess of my life, and I don't know how to get it back on the rails again. I don't have a girlfriend, the wife's taken the kiddie and I don't have any mates. There's not very much that I do have, to be frank about it. It's lonely.

– Maybe if I get to Waddell Moor it'll be a new life. My mam says I'm not all that old, I can start a new life if I go to Waddell Moor and begin again. But I don't think I want to stop in the mines. There isn't the feeling that it's a good place to be, with a good future to it. But other jobs are hard to come by in this part of the world: you've got to think hard before you put yourself out of a job.

My long and happy retirement
Bernard Wilkinson

His house was a large and comfortably furnished modern
bungalow at the side of a green in a private estate ten
miles away from the village. He was a very large and com-
fortably furnished man, burly and with bright blue eyes.
He wore a sleeveless roll-necked canary yellow pullover,
a check shirt, check trousers, and light grey leather
shoes.

– I won't switch the telly off, I'll turn the sound down
though: I want to keep an eye on it, I'm waiting for the
boxing. He's good this young McGuigan lad isn't he? Long
time since we've had one like him.

I've been nearly twenty years a miner, and I'm bloody
glad to be getting away from it. There's a lot will tell you
coal mining isn't what it used to be, that all the heart's
gone out of it. If they do, that means they're Union men
through and through. All that's gone out of coal mining is
the stranglehold the Union had on it, and that can only be
good. For years there was just a few people who kept it
under their thumb. Now those people have been shown
the error of their ways, and I don't think that's bad. The
main thing that's been wrong with this country for years is
the trades unions. Thatcher's seen them off once and for
all in my opinion. They've had it coming to them, they
had it for years where they were in clover. Course they
don't like it now that the tables have been turned, but
those bad old days are over. I think there's more chance
now of a decent lot of men coming in, and we'll have
the industry run properly. MacGregor's running it as a
business, not as an organisation of cushy jobs for the boys,
and that can only be good.

I'm retiring early next year when I'm fifty. To go early

and be leaving an opening for a younger man, that was my intention all the way through. I get good redundancy money and me and the wife we've been sensible and looked after our money. We've got this nice house, our daughter's going to college, and what's to come now is what I've worked for twenty years for, my long and happy retirement, thank you very much. I'm going to enjoy every single bloody minute of it.

Yes, I was one of those who was against the strike from the start. I think everyone had an inkling it might be coming, but we thought there'd be a national ballot. Like there should have been. Only Arthur Scargill, he's a man for confrontation, not like Joe Gormley who believed in a bit of give and take. Gormley was a great man and he did a lot for the Union: Scargill's a small man and he's done more harm to the industry than anyone ever before or since. I think it won't be long before everyone comes to see it that way and to see what Scargill was after, which was power for himself. He didn't have no sympathy for the working miner at all, he'd have kept them out on strike until they dropped dead from starvation rather than climb down himself. He let it run on and on, long after it was obvious to everyone he'd no hope at all of winning. But that sort of thing's always been typical of the NUM: the men who are at the top of it are more concerned with their own power and prestige than anything else. Mind you, I supported the Union through the 1972 and 1974 strikes because those were for better wages and working conditions.

When I first went in the mines I was thirty-two. I had a time before that as a seaman, but I come from an army family really. Basically it's an army thing that if you work hard and keep your nose clean you'll get on, so you might say I come from a disciplined background. I've never been brought up to regard myself as one who was better than other people. I think all I had in the way of a temperament was itchy feet. I liked going to different places and seeing different parts of the world, and it was that that gave me a broader outlook than a lot of men who've only ever been down a coal mine all their lives. The way of life's quite good, but it's always been a bit too clannish for me. If your face fitted you were the first to be considered for the better jobs underground when the Union was dividing them up. But if it was a choice between a man who did his work and did it properly, and a man who didn't do it so well but gave up a fair bit of time to letting his mouth off at the Union meetings, it would be usually the second one who got it, other things being equal.

There's more than once in the years that I've been there I'd like to have come out of the pit if I could have got something else. I often thought of trying for one of these jobs you read about in the Middle East, the Persian Gulf or somewhere of that sort. You go and work for a short time there and make a lot of money, then you come home and enjoy the fruits of your labour. You don't get any of all this union rubbish out there: everyone's too busy making money for themselves. And they don't have unions because what's there to complain about? I was saying to the wife the other night, she agreed with me that if I'd done that sort of job when I intended ten years ago, we'd have been a lot more comfortable now. I wouldn't have minded being on my own out there, you could get a nice house with the job. And native servants and all that business, they're only too glad to come and work for you, and you didn't have to pay them a lot. People have got fancy ideas now in this country about that sort of thing. The wife's got a job, a good one: she's a secretary in a company and she doesn't mind being her boss's servant. Sometimes she has to be like a waitress when they have board meetings of directors: well I say a waitress, but bringing in the tea and biscuits is about the extent of it. She doesn't mind doing that, why should she? Her boss always gives her a bit extra for doing it at the end of the day if she's had to stop late, so everyone's happy.

She's always worked, always had a job. Between us

we've bought the house and we've seen to it our daughter
was always nicely clothed It's going to cost us a lot now
she's going away to college, but you don't mind making
sacrifices for your children, not if you feel in the end it's
going to lead to something good for her. She's doing
business studies: she's a bright girl, she ought to get
on and perhaps make a lot more money than her father's
ever done, and I'd be the first to be proud of her if she
did.

– We didn't really get far on the subject of the strike the
other night did we, no. I think I told you I'd had enough
after the first day because I could see it plain for what it
was: Scargill's personal strike, that's all. I didn't agree with
him, and I didn't agree with his way of going about things.
I'm no man's servant, but the Coal Board have never done
no harm to me: if the Government was saying it couldn't
afford to go on running uneconomic mines, we should have
all buckled down to it without all the whimpering there
was. Mrs Thatcher was trying to run a country, not something for charity, so there'll always be some who has to
make sacrifices. I went to the Board the very first week of
the strike: I told them I didn't want to be out on strike,
and as soon as they were ready they could count on me
for being one of the first to go back. In fact I told them if
they wanted someone to set an example, I would be the
one to do it. I wouldn't have been frightened of walking
through a picket line, never mind going in a bus with
dozens of police all round it. If only enough of us had got
together at the beginning and done that, showed the Union
we'd no time for what was going on and walked in, then
there'd have been no trouble. All the mines would have
been working again in a few weeks. The men were frightened of the Union, that's all: they'd dare less to go against
what the Union said than they would against what the Coal
Board said. And there was men in the Union, there still
are, who play on other men's fears and take advantage of

them for their own personal political quarrels with the bosses. That's all I'm saying: and it's true.

There was men working all through the strike on safety cover: men were going in every day in small teams, going underground and doing whatever little bits were necessary to preserve the mine in working order and keep it safe until working was to start again. And it was the Union who picked the men who were to be allowed to do that: there was a lot of favouritism there about that, I can tell you.

After three months I was, I was completely fed up with it. All that shouting and rioting going on, seeing it every night on the telly, I was disgusted with it. I even talked with the wife of going down to Nottinghamshire a while, seeing if I could get a job there where a lot of the pits were working, and her perhaps following me. It was something we seriously considered, but nothing came of it. I just wanted to work that was all, and I didn't see anyone had the right to stop me. I'll tell you this, there was more than half the men at Red Hill pit, if they were going to be honest about it they felt the same way. You get that lot in the Welfare Hall down there, they're only a hundred out of nearly a thousand. Those hundred are the noisy ones, the ones who're always shouting about everything. They take a vote for a strike, and everyone puts their hand up except a few, and so then they say 'There you are, we're solid for a strike.' Course they're solid, because they're the ones who've turned out for the meeting. But no one goes round and asks all of the men what they think. I guarantee that if at any time Scargill had taken a vote throughout the whole membership of the NUM – I don't mean just that part of it which goes to meetings, but the whole membership – he'd never have got a majority. I shouldn't think there was ten per cent really wanted that strike. If you look at the figures, I doubt if a quarter of the Union members ever turned up to a meeting, let alone supported a motion for strike action.

When they started offering the Christmas bonus for those who would go back to work in the November, I was one of the first to get in touch with the Coal Board and tell them they could count on me. I didn't see why my Christmas and our family's Christmas and a lot of other people's Christmases should be ruined, just because of a handful of hotheads. I told them at the Board that was how I felt, and that I was damn sure a lot of other men felt the same. The Board said they didn't know how they were going to get Red Hill working, because of the Union people being so strong there. They asked me would I consider going to work temporarily at another pit, where they thought they could probably get more than half the work force in. They said they were fairly sure if they did the rest would follow. I said yes, I was willing.

They laid on buses to pick us up at various points that we could get to, and so we all went in to work at Waddell Moor. My particular place for reporting was the police station here, but they had to be a bit careful with some of the others in case it was found out where they were to be collected. We got the mine back in operation very quickly, within three weeks the wheels were turning and we were getting coal out. We worked right over until the New Year, and then after everyone started to come back. I've stayed there ever since.

The pickets tried to stop us of course. Just before Christmas they organised a big blockade. But the police got wind of it, and they were ready for them. There were sticks and rocks and God knows what, but we got in. Then the same thing the next day, and the day after that. There were some arrests but gradually after that we were more or less left alone. The bullies hadn't succeeded in getting their way, and things went along fairly straight-forwardly.

When the strike was called off in the March, I thought I might go back to Red Hill. I don't know how many of them knew I'd been working or where, or for how long.

That was my business, not theirs. Anyway I'm a big chap and I can look after myself. Nobody's ever fronted me up and they'd soon learn their mistake if they did. I'm not frightened of a fight.

I've done nothing that I should be ashamed of, and I'd do exactly the same thing again. The only difference this time would be I'd do it a lot earlier. I'd have led a march back down to work through the picket line if they'd let me: I would, and I can't put it any squarer than that. I've always been a bit of an awkward one all my life, I don't like other people telling me what I can do and what I can't. I make up my own mind, and if I want to go to work I'd like to see any bugger in the Union try to stop me.

– The way I see it going now is there'll be a very big shake-up. In the Union, I'm talking about: and that's something that's bound to be good in the long run for the coal industry. The new Union that's been formed, the Union of Democratic Miners, I think that's a very good thing. In a free country like we've got, a man ought to have his freedom of choice. If he thinks his own union's no good then he should be able to join another one. Or he shouldn't even be in a union at all if he doesn't want to be. There's no point to me joining the UDM now, but I would if I were a younger man. It started in Nottingham because it was mostly the Nottingham men who kept on working, which they were entitled to. They were getting better money than we were, but I said good luck to them. You couldn't expect them to put themselves out of work, especially not if it was their pits which were not in danger. The Nottingham coalfield is a good one, with a lot of modern plant and investment and tons of coal, I think it would be a good place for someone to work. I could very well go and live somewhere down there next year, the wife's got family in those parts.

I don't want to stay on round here now: a shame when you look at this lovely house we've got, all saved up for and paid for. But when you're retired I think you want something to do. I'm a bit of a handyman so I wouldn't mind taking on a new place and doing it up. Like I was saying to you the other night, my own business is my own business: but there are blokes in this part of the world, if they found out some of the things I've been telling to you . . . well I won't say they'd make it hot for me because they don't come much round here, but it would mean there were certain clubs and pubs in the area that I wouldn't be much welcome in. I'm not frightened, but I've been sickened in the last few years with what's been going on in the Union. There's a really violent vicious feeling that's come into things nowadays, and it never used to be like it before. So when I'm retired, I want to enjoy it, I don't want to be having to keep looking over my shoulder all the time.

The wife's not keen on moving and giving up her job, because she enjoys it. And she says with Karen going away which she probably will do in a year or so, it's going to be very lonely for her without her. But I expect she'll settle down, and she'll be nearer her family: she'll come to it in time. Myself, I fancy taking up golf or something of that sort, I can see myself on a golf course. I've never played it in my life, but I'd think it's one of those things that if you settle down and put your hand to it, you can get yourself good enough to enjoy it. Another thing I wouldn't mind doing, I've often had this in my mind too, is I'd like to collect stamps. I suppose it's the different countries in the world, looking up in an atlas where they all are and that sort of thing that appeals to me. And they tell you don't they it's a good investment as well, so I wouldn't be throwing my money away.

I've had a decent life, the wife and I have never wanted for anything in the way of material possessions and friends. I don't think anyone could be prouder of his daughter than

I am. There's not a day I regret, and I reckon next year's the right time for me to get out. New Zealand is a place I wouldn't mind going to, they tell me it's nice there. Who knows?

I'd say it was a place full of laughter
Tom Day

On a cold and darkening winter afternoon, his big old detached house in the middle of the village was a place of welcomingly lit downstairs windows, its inside warm and bright. His wife brought a tea tray with china cups and saucers, biscuits, and a piled-high plate of hot buttered cheese scones into the high-ceilinged sitting room. He was a quietly spoken man in a plain dark lounge suit.

– I retired a few years ago and at that time I was fifty-nine, far and away the oldest man in the pit then. I started in the mines in 1941 when I was seventeen. I was articled to a mining engineer and my first job was as an under manager at Milford Main. Then I was what they call spare for six months, going to different places wherever they wanted me, then eventually I came here as deputy manager, and some years after that I became general manager until I retired. And oh, for me that was the great day: it'd always been my ambition right from a boy to be Manager of Red Hill. There was nowhere else would do, that was where I wanted to be. So it was, when I became manager it was a very proud day. It had always had such a reputation, had Red Hill. Before the war you know, it was the largest pit in the Empire in terms of production, and in the sixties it employed over 3,000 men.

It always used to be that the line of command in the mines had always been from within the industry. Men felt, they were encouraged to feel, that if they wanted to they could become managers themselves one day: and it was true, a lot did, I know any amount who have. And we used to reckon that at Red Hill we had the best relations between the Board and the men of almost any pit in the country. It was something everybody could be very proud of, and everybody *was* very proud of. I don't mind saying

so myself, but I don't think anyone would contradict it.
And particularly there was always very good relations with
the Union. At one time the Red Hill Lodge Chairman was
a member of the Communist party: but he was a good man
to work with, and very moderate in his outlook. Him and
me, we got on well. Because you see after all we were
really the same kind of people underneath. The workers
were my own people, and I was their own, and we all knew
one another: and not only that but our fathers had known
one another, and in some cases our grandfathers had been
the same too. I would know for instance a young lad and
I'd be able to say to him 'I knew your father when he
worked here.' There were occasions when we'd had three
generations of one family in the pit. And it gives it a special
feeling: for the pit, for the job and for all the people
working there one for another.

In its early days ninety-nine per cent of Red Hill workers
lived here within this village. Peterlee was built as a kind
of overflow for all the old little villages around here, to
give miners better housing. But a lot of them went there
and they didn't like it, so they came back again because
they preferred it round here. Peterlee was meant to give
people new homes, and when they'd left here many of the
old houses round about were pulled down. Peterlee? Well
he was a leader you know, a famous miners' leader was
Peter Lee. I just remember him: he was a kind of God-like
figure with a beard. Somebody introduced me to him when
I was a little lad. He was a check weighman at a colliery,
they used to say he was a right fighting man on the slag
heap on a Sunday afternoon. To have a town named after
you, from being a coal miner, that's not a bad memorial
is it?

So with the new housing over there and so on, over the
years there's been a lot of changes in the village. Chiefly
with old houses being pulled down, and there used to be
three cinemas here but they've gone. The pubs haven't
changed much, but it was always more of a place for clubs
for the working men rather than pubs.

One disadvantage it did have, and still does to some extent, is with people who work together and nearly everyone living in the same place, it can sometimes happen that a little trouble can be talked up into a big trouble. When work's finished you can't cut yourself off from it or get away from it: whereas when people live in different places I think that can sometimes put more of a perspective to things for them. There's arguments on both sides, because on the other hand at work there's more of a community feeling, as I was saying.

– A lot of people say that if Red Hill pit is closed, that'll be the death knell of the village as a community. Well as far as that's concerned, if it does happen we shall have to see: I'm not so sure myself. There are a fair number of villages round here that at one time were centred on their own pits. When they closed and the men transferred to go and work at other pits, they came back home to their own villages where they lived to spend their money. What's beginning to look different now though is that there's such a high unemployment rate in this area they just won't be able to go on offering them transfers. Or if they do, you can see that face workers, power loaders and the rest of the high-paid men, they won't want to go to other pits and find themselves almost being datal workers, even if their earnings are protected for the first three years like they say they will be. They'll be getting all the most boring jobs and there's bound to be a limit on the number of power loaders who can be accommodated at any one pit. This transfer business is not quite as simple as some people would like to make out. I was talking to a man in one of the clubs the other day, he was telling me he'd been to a pit where he'd heard there were vacancies and they told him they were reserving them all for men from one particular pit over the other side that was closing. I think a lot of people are going to leave the industry altogether over the next few years, but what they're going to do no one knows. If I could tell you a solution to that, I reckon I'd be worth a high position in the industry or the Government wouldn't I?

You see at the heart of the problem is the fact that coal mining is an extractive industry. Like I told you, Red Hill had been a very big pit, but by the time I left its labour force was down to 1,300 men, and now it's 800. Seams get worked out, and there isn't a person in the world'd go so far as to suggest there's any point in keeping open any pit when it's reached that stage. If you look back over the years since nationalisation, somewhere in the region of 900 pits altogether have been closed in this country. It wasn't a policy – not in those days – to run down the coal industry. It was just the simple reality that if there was no more coal, that had to be the end of that pit. The Union accepted it, the men accepted it. But of course two things were different, there was careful preparation, and there were offers of new jobs. Not like now when we've reached a totally different situation, and it's one of such bitter conflict and disagreement that no one at all can tell what the ultimate outcome will be. In all my life I've never known a time like this, with so many divisions, and such deep divisions, between management and men. There were troubles in 1972 and 1974, but when the strikes were over the bad feelings were over with them. Fences were mended and bridges were rebuilt, and that was the end of it.

But this time it's very different. The strike was such a very long runner, and both sides got more and more deeply entrenched. There was a great deal more media attention given to it too, than there's ever been before. And it was unfortunately nearly all of it concentrated on the violence. Up here to anyone who knew anything about it it was ridiculous: you'd have thought there was fighting all day long every day, outside every pit. All right yes there was some trouble, but only some: it seemed to a lot of people you could almost say the media fostered it. They put it over in such a way that both the miners and the police – well I won't say they went looking for it, but they were being conditioned almost to expect it and be ready for it.

What you might call the trigger point got higher and higher all the time as a result if you see what I mean.

And it was always being put over too as a personal confrontation between Arthur Scargill, Ian MacGregor and Margaret Thatcher, and all three of them were very ready to let it become one. As soon as one appeared on the television, the other one expected equal time to refute the points the first one had made. This didn't do anything at all to help reasonableness prevail. All of them, they were all striking attitudes, making of threats, issuing statements that whoever else backed down, it wasn't going to be them. Well honestly you know, I could never have settled arguments and differences between management and union or anyone else in that kind of atmosphere, no one could. Those things did nothing whatever to help finding a solution. I wasn't the only one who felt sometimes there ought to be a complete clampdown on all news and pictures of all kinds, for a long long period: till the people involved had got together and worked the thing out properly between them, in the way it's been done in the past. A quiet word here, a meeting there: now and again some big rows, but not in public, surely not. That's the only way ever that people who are opposed to each other'll find any sort of meeting ground and eventual solution.

Oh well, I suppose it's easy for someone like me to talk like this now, because I wasn't involved. I retired very shortly before the strike began and so I just missed it. No I wouldn't say I was glad about it particularly. I suppose everybody thinks when they've spent their whole life with something, like I did with the coal industry and its people at all levels, that no one understands it like they do, and they could bring something or contribute something to finding a settlement. I don't mean on my own or anything of that sort, but I was sorry to see what went on. I would really have liked to have been there, being one of those who was trying to reach a solution. I did, I regretted I wasn't in a position to be involved. I don't know necessarily that the Board would have allowed me to play much part, and I wouldn't have expected to do at manager level. But I'd like to have been there, and trying. I don't know either whether the Board'll be all that pleased I go on talking about it in this fashion afterwards: but of course after all now I'm only talking as a private individual.

Summing it up, it seems to me there were two main things wrong about the strike and its aftermath. This is only my opinion, but I think the first one is it was altogether wrong that at a certain stage the Union didn't have a ballot. They should have done, and I think they had a chance that if they put their case over properly, they might have got a majority of miners in support of what they were trying to do. It never occurred to me like I'm sure it didn't to a lot of people, that they'd carry on as long as they did without having a ballot. It's not for me to tell them how to run their affairs, but some would say it could have had a lot of advantages for the Union whatever the result of a ballot had turned out to be. If they'd got a majority for strike action, then of course they'd have had enormous public sympathy and even more than that, a great deal of public support. I mean look at how much they got *without* a ballot. So I think in the long run, or even possibly in the short run, the Coal Board would in the end have had to have come to the bargaining table and make some fairly extensive concessions to meet the Union's demands. But as it was, they could take shelter behind the fact there hadn't been a ballot: and they could persist like they did persist in refusing any kind of negotiation at all.

And if the Union had held a ballot and hadn't got a majority, well even that would have given the Union the opportunity to withdraw and back down with a bit of dignity, and stay alive to fight on another day. As they say, there's no great disgrace in losing a battle: it doesn't mean the end of hope, and it doesn't mean you've lost all serious chance of winning the war. I don't see how the unions ever thought for one moment they could win, because right from the start they were so disadvantaged in every way. The coal stocks had been built up, the strike was begun coming out of winter instead of going into it, the day after day reporting of it was totally unfavourable to them all the way through. To my mind they should have seen the light long before they did. But they made serious mistakes: and again though it's not for me to say, I think it's going to be a very long time before they recover. I think you can see that in the setting up of this new breakaway union, the Union of Democratic Miners: tremendous damage has been done to the NUM and all in all the end of the strike was a sad day for them.

But that said, the other thing that now strikes me as equally wrong is that now when the strike is over, it's so much a case of to the victor the spoils. The Coal Board seems to be going absolutely on the rampage. They seem to think they can do exactly what they like with the men. They behave in any way they like, and their whole attitude towards them is that they've 'won'. If they do see things like that, I think it's a very short-sighted view. The coal industry has always been one in which the human relationship side of things was very important and something to be very proud of. You can't just trample all over it and pretend it doesn't matter. The strike brought great hardship and difficulty to many many thousands of people and now it's over it doesn't mean there's no room for compassion and forgiveness. The next few years are going to be hard enough for everyone concerned to make up what they've lost, without adding complete loss of dignity for them as well to it.

– I miss the pit, I miss the mining life, I really do. There was something special about coal mining. It was a man's life, and I miss the whole atmosphere and friendship at the place of work. There was times when to be the manager was lonely. It had to be. You were the final arbiter of disputes and arguments and problems at the pit, and you always had to try your best to strike a balance that was fair to all sides. And you could only do that if all sides felt you had no favourites: so you tried your best to find what was fair between one person and another and one side and another. To do that, you had to have people's respect: and the only way you could get it was by showing them you were an independent and fair-minded person. But you weren't given respect: you had to earn it.

It was true, and I think a lot of people who were there at the same time would back me up saying it, that at Red Hill pit we had a good workplace, a real friendly pit, and one that was just a little bit special. Because I enjoyed it, I wasn't a strict nine till five man as the manager. There were occasions when I was called in late at night, and perhaps sometimes didn't get out again till midday the following day. The working conditions weren't always comfortable: but like everyone else when I was down the pit, I was more than prepared, I was ready and willing, to take my share of the physical difficulties. There were places down there where you were standing in water pouring all over you from the roof at times. Lots of men wouldn't have put up with it, but if it was necessary Red Hill men did and I'd join them in it. It's an incredible thing but even under conditions like that, time and time again when although we were in difficulties and perhaps even sometimes in danger, we were not only working hard to set something right, but we were all of us laughing and joking about it while we were doing it. It was a good happy pit, and in my recollection of it I'd say it was a place full of laughter.

But I don't believe it's that no longer, not now. And knowledge of that you know is something very saddening now.

Not all honey and spice

George Driver
Cliff Marshall
Alan Whitfield
Gary Neil

George Driver

– I was a miner, only now I have to say I'm a permanently sacked miner, one of the great unemployed. I'm thirty-four and I've been at the pit since I was sixteen, that's eighteen years. I'm married with three kids – the eldest one's a girl of eleven, then I've another girl seven and a boy who's now just two this week.

It's very hard for me, now not to be a pit man. I was dismissed fourteen months ago during the strike. I was on the picket line not at my own pit but one of the Yorkshire ones. Some days there was a lot of fighting between the police and us: drivers drove their lorries out past us, carrying coal and waving £10 notes at us in their hands. One day it came to it that we stopped one of the trucks, and the driver was pulled out. Four of us – well we did, we roughed him up quite a lot: I look back on it and I know we went too far. I'm not saying this to excuse us, but we'd been in a bit of a scrap already with the police that day and our tempers were up, and they did, things got out of hand. The result of it was I was charged with grievous bodily harm and assault on the police. I was kept in the police station two days, and they roughed me up and all, because I'd whacked one of their men and damaged his face.

I didn't think it was going to be as serious as it turned out, I thought they were just going to make an example of us. But when we came up in court a week later, I got fined £200 and given a twelve-month sentence suspended two years. The other three men with me didn't get as heavy a whack as I did, because the police said I was the ringleader. A week later at home I'd been out of the house

all morning and when I got back the wife said someone
had called from the pit and left an envelope for me. It was
my notice, they'd sacked me on the grounds of misconduct.
They said there was no appeal, I was paid off with just my
holiday money: £100 and that was it.

My life's been nothing ever since. I thought at the end
of the strike there was going to be an amnesty, I think
everybody thought that, but so far the Coal Board hasn't
shifted an inch. I went down to the pit last week to see
some of my mates for a chat, and I went into the pit
canteen with them for a cup of tea. The Under Manager
came in, and he come straight up to me at the table where
I was, he knows me, and he said 'Out you, this canteen's
for employees of the Coal Board only.'

In the last year all I've done is kept my allotment and
other than that nothing. I can't see much prospect of
another job, not now I've got this record. I've been for a
couple of small jobs, one as a van driver and one cleaning
up in a factory, both very low pay. For the van driver there
was another forty men after it, and for the cleaning-up job
I think it was thirty. They asked me at both of them why
I'd left the pit: I had to tell them I'd been sacked and what
for, so I didn't stand much chance in competition with all
those others who hadn't even got records.

One thing which doesn't count for me with the Board
though is that at the first meeting we had at the pit to see
if we should strike, I voted against it because I didn't think
we should. It was only after people talked to me and
explained what it was all about I came round to thinking
it was right. I wasn't a bad man, at least I don't think
myself I was a bad man. Only a bit of a hothead if you
like. I've always had a short temper, it made us very angry
those drivers coming through out of the pit gates mocking
us. It had been a bad morning for us with the police shoving
us about. Up till then I'd been one of the ones who just
shouted and waved my fists, but I'd never used violence
on no one.

It's a high price to pay at my age, to think you can't see

yourself being back in a job for the rest of your life. Unemployment being as much as it is, you don't stand a big chance of a job if all the experience you've got behind you is coal mining and the Coal Board tell you that they're never going to employ you no more. It wouldn't make no difference wherever I went, if I moved house and went to some other coalfield it'd still be the Coal Board I'd have to face. They've given some men their jobs back, but those were mostly the ones who were convicted of stealing coal. I don't know of no one with a violence conviction who they've taken on again yet. But I think they ought to, I think they ought to make a gesture of that kind. But they're getting rid of men, not taking more on, so prospects are pretty poor.

The wife says she accepts it's going to be a life on the dole for us for ever more. That's a hard thing to swallow when you're fit and healthy, and I feel I've been punished twice – once by the court and then again by the Coal Board. I look at the wife and kids sometimes and I wonder what the future's going to be, if there's going to be a future, any future at all. I don't drink, I don't smoke, we go without everything that we can and the kids miss out on a lot of things too. I don't want to think it's going to go on like that for years, but I don't see how it's going to change. One day things are bound to get better, the wife says. But I feel though I've very badly let them down: that's what I feel.

Cliff Marshall

– You're talking to someone who'd tell you he's thirty years old and a man on the scrap heap with no hope at all. I'm married with three children, and if you'd come to talk to me before the strike I was a power loader on the top rate of pay and with everything going for me.

I was another of those like George that you've been talking to, at the first meeting I voted against us coming out on strike. Those who put their hands up were only about six altogether, and I was one of them and George was another. But I'd worked at the pit for nine years and I stayed solid with my mates: they all felt the time had come to take a stand. We weren't misled by Arthur Scargill or anyone else: he was right in everything what he said. When people say you've been misled, it's like they're saying you can't think for yourselves.

What I did to get into trouble was I painted the side of a scab's house. He wasn't a scab at our pit, he lived on an estate over the other side of Peterlee, he was scabbing somewhere else. So several of us went over one night with pots of paint, and put it in big letters on the outside of his house so everyone could see what he was. And we also painted out his windows. They said it was a bad case because it was night, he and his family were all in bed and they were too terrified to come out and do anything about it. But we didn't hurt no one, it wasn't an attack on a person. Only the house belonged to the National Coal Board, and we got done by them for criminal damage. I didn't know the man, and to this day I still don't know why the police came round to my house. But they did, and when they looked in my dustbin they found an empty one of the big cans of paint. It was the red colour exactly the same as we'd painted the word 'Scab' on the wall in.

I got a sentence of two months' imprisonment. I was expecting a fine or something of that sort, definitely not prison. I'd got one previous conviction years ago when I was a lad, sixteen: that was assault and I got a £20 fine. The magistrates said they were going to make an example of us, it was to be a deterrent for others. I was in Durham Gaol all told ten weeks and while I was there I lost a stone in weight. The wife brought the kiddies to see me twice but it was very upsetting for all of us, afterwards I wished they hadn't been.

But I thought at least that was the end of it then. I

thought if you were in trouble and you went to prison, you were supposed to start again when you came out with a clean sheet. The strike was still on when I came out so I didn't go back to work no more than anyone else did till it was over. But when I went in on the first day of the return back to work, on the Tuesday, one of the Under Managers came and said to me 'You can't go down the pit.' He sent me home and told me I was to wait until I heard. Two days later I did hear, they sent me my notice.

I've got a feeling the police had it in for me; they knew I'd been one of those who'd been active on the picket lines outside a lot of pits in the area: they regarded me as a troublemaker. Somebody must have informed on me about the painting business, because otherwise the police wouldn't have come round just to my house: I was the only one in the street they came to for a search.

No, from here I don't know where I'm going to go. It's very hard to see what sort of a future there can be for me. I can't get a job with a prison record: there's lots of men who can't get a job who haven't been in prison, so I reckon there's not much hope for me. The Union tell us they'll keep fighting to try and get us reinstated, I'm not the only one they're fighting on behalf of. But I can't see it happening, not with things the way they are. I haven't given up hope entirely, I don't want to take another job even if I could find one, because I want to keep myself available for pit work. I'm not one for hanging around so I don't really know what the next step should be. The wife and I don't talk about it much: not now, we used to but it got us down, so we try not to think about it. I mean I did what I did, but I'd like the gaol sentence wiped off because it's over now. I'm ready if they give me a chance to make a fresh start. I even went to the Coal Board and said to them if they'd let me, I'd go back and repaint the house for them. But of course they wouldn't listen to that. So where to go or what to do I've no idea. You wouldn't think that at thirty you could end up in this sort of a mess in your life.

I wasn't an idle man never, I was a hard worker and I think I was a good one. I've never been in trouble in my life except for that once when I was a kid of sixteen. And once I got caught with some lads, pinching. But I got let off that. I haven't been let off about this: but what I'm saying about is it's over and I ought to start equal again in the Board's eyes with the others. They're offering transfers or redundancies to other men, but there's nothing of that sort they're offering me.

Alan Whitfield

– I'd say I'm a very happy-go-lucky sort of a person, tries to keep smiling, know what I mean? But it's difficult: I try to keep cheerful about things, but they're not very funny, nothing's funny just now.

I'm forty-two. I've been in it since I was fifteen, like my father before me, and I've two brothers in the pit as well. When I was coming up to leaving school I remember my dad said 'If you want to know what it's like, go out to the coalhouse at twelve o'clock at night and crawl around in there for a bit with a candle, that'll give you an idea of what it's like.' He was right!

I'm divorced, and I've got one girl eleven who lives with the ex-wife. I'd say definitely it was the strike caused the divorce. The wife wasn't sympathetic to the miners and we were always rowing about it: she kept telling me I was a lazy bugger and ought to get back to work. I used to go out of the house to get away from her, and then one day I hit her once too often and she pissed off to her mother's. We'd been married thirteen years, it'd not been a happy marriage more or less from the start. Although I've said to you it was the strike caused it, to be honest I think we'd have divorced anyway in the end.

After the wife'd left I was drinking quite a bit then, a

lot more than usual. Seven pints of beer's usually my limit, but there was nothing to stay in the house for and I did have a right skinful once or twice. I'd voted for the strike right from the beginning because I thought it was right: I'm a Scargill man and he's always been straight with us. If he said something was true, you could take it without any quibble it was true: and he was the first person to stand up to the Thatcher woman for a long time. They was all shit scared of her in British Steel works, British Leyland, all the other places where she broke the strikes. But Scargill wasn't: he was the only man in the country who'd got the guts to stand up with her.

I went and did a bit of picketing along with some of the other lads at different places, sometimes down in Yorkshire, sometimes in Nottinghamshire. I got arrested here though in this part of the world, at an open-cast working. It was late one night and a driver turned up with his lorry to go in. We tried to argue with him and turn him back, but all he did was kept revving his engine as though he was going to drive over us. Eventually we pulled him out, and I had a stick of wood in my hand and I belted him with it. It wasn't something I should have done, I realised that as soon as it'd been done. We all came back to the village as quick as we could in one of our blokes' cars, and we went in the Welfare Hall for a game of snooker. The police were on to us pretty quick, they came in only just a few minutes later and pulled us out and took us back over to their local station.

They took me in and sat me in a room on a chair, and one questioned me and the other one gave me a belt when they didn't like my answers. What I was saying all along was the same thing, I didn't know what they were talking about and I'd been in a pub all night. They said the driver had recognised me, he'd known my name. I couldn't work out how that'd come about, because he wasn't someone I knew. I think I was often one of the prominent ones on the picket lines, and they'd have probably said something to him like 'It sounds like that bugger Whitfield.' This fleck of white hair I've got above my temple here, it might have been that gave me away. Anyway.

They was hitting us and hitting us, and in the end they broke me and I admitted it was me. I didn't give them the names of the others who were with me though. They told me it'd go easier for me if I did, but I wasn't going to fall for that. The lorry driver we'd pulled out of his cab had to have seventeen stitches, so I got done for GBH and the offensive weapon, which is how they described the stick. So I got a sentence of nine months' suspended imprisonment, and a fine of £200.

When they let me out of the police station the next morning there was a man on the street who said he was a photographer for one of the national daily papers. He asked me if he could take pictures of my face and promised me he'd send copies to me, but he never did. They didn't print the pictures in their newspaper either.

I think it was about a couple of months I had to wait before my court case came up. As soon as it was over they came round the same day from the Coal Board and said they didn't want to see me again, and gave me my notice. They said it was because the assault had been perpetrated on Coal Board property. But it wasn't: the open-cast working was a private yard, and the lorry driver trying to go in worked for a private contractor. I don't see what it had to do with the Coal Board, I think they're being vindictive because they knew I was an active man on the picket lines.

It's hard for me to see what there is for me to do now. I don't see myself getting a job back with the Coal Board again. Still you keep smiling don't you? Perhaps I could take up a life of crime or something, that seems about the only future for me. I did ask a bloke about it in a pub, he was supposed to be a bit of a villain, least that's what they said. But he said I was too well known now, and I got caught too easy, I wouldn't be any use to him.

If there was one thing I could change and go back on

and start again, it's that I wish it all hadn't happened, the strike had never took place and I was back with the wife again.

Gary Neil

– To get a new government in is the only hope so far as I can see it, for Labour to come in and give everyone an amnesty. If they was to say bygones were bygones and all those that wanted to could start again with a clean sheet, that's the only hope I can see. Apart from that I don't see anything at all, everything's very bleak.

I'm twenty-five, I'm single and I live at home with my mam and I keep pigeons. I've two sisters that're married: one of them's husband's a miner, he's in the Nottingham-shire coalfield and he's one of the ones that's doing all right. My father died last year in the middle of the strike, and my mam said my sister wasn't to bring her husband to our house while it was going on. She felt very bitter about it. She said if Tracey's father had been alive he'd have had a stand up fight with her husband and set about him for being one who didn't stand by the Union.

I came to work at Red Hill when they were having that big recruiting drive seven or eight years ago. I was seventeen and I'd tried a few odd jobs when I left school, but I couldn't settle to anything. I didn't much fancy the idea of working underground, but once I got in the pit there wasn't no choice. I was on the bank in the timber shed one day and the Under Manager come to me and he said 'You – Monday down the pit' and that was it. It was all right when you got used to it, it wasn't as bad as they tell you. I was mostly to do with the cleaning and setting of machinery: it was a boring job but not badly paid.

When the strike come on, I was one of those who wasn't really for it. I thought unless we were solid everywhere

we'd never succeed. The way I looked at it, there wasn't
much chance of that and all that'd happen would be the
Union would tear itself in half. But if you're in the Union
and the Union says strike, you strike when the majority of
your mates have voted for that. I took my turn on the
picket line, and I went to one or two other places round
the area. I'm not a rowdy sort of person and I was never
intending to get into trouble, not attacking lorry drivers
and things of that sort which some others have done.

You might not believe this, a lot of people wouldn't, but
it's true – one day we got a tip-off from a policeman that
the next day they were going to try and get a miner into
the pit through a back way at Waddell Moor. That was
one of the pits in the area where there was a feeling for
going back to work. I think the Coal Board's idea was if
they got one man in there, then some of the others might
follow.

So some of us all got down there early next morning,
and we got into the pit yard through a fence at the side.
And it was true, they did bring a man in through the back
way in a car and we all jumped on them and there was a
scrap. Then they opened the front gate and let some police
vans in, so some more of our men got in as well. It was all
like a battlefield. The police were thumping us and booting
us and everyone was shouting and swearing. Me and three
other lads ran to the car, and we pushed it over. The police
arrested us and put handcuffs on us, and they put us in
a van and took us off. We were charged with assault,
threatening words and behaviour, and criminal damage.

I was put in Durham Gaol on remand for ten days, and
then I got bailed. The conditions were that I obeyed a
curfew and wasn't out of my house after seven o'clock at
night, that I did no more picketing, and that I didn't set
foot anywhere on any NCB property. This was in the
August: then they kept renewing the bail, and it got to
two weeks before Christmas before the case was finally
heard. They'd dropped the assault and the threatening
words and behaviour, so the only charge left was criminal

damage. I got four months for that, right before Christmas. So I had my Christmas day dinner in Durham Gaol, then I got sent on to a semi-open prison, then about a week after that I got my notice from the Coal Board.

There was three other miners in there, the open prison, and the screws were right bastards to all of us. One day a truck come in, a big truck with a tarpaulin over it, and they told us to unload it. When they took the cover off it was coal inside, and they started jeering and shouting 'Come on you coal miners, let's see you shift this fucking coal.' We refused to touch it, we said we wasn't going to move coal anywhere for anybody. They put us up in front of the governor, and he said we'd lose our remission if we disobeyed an order. The strike was still on at the time, and we said that the Union would black us and not let us have our jobs back again if we moved any coal. I think we were bluffing, we weren't as certain as we made out. Anyway he let it drop, we didn't move the coal, we didn't lose remission, and we heard no more about it.

I've been to see the Coal Board three times since I came out, and they say every time that they're not going to re-employ me. I don't see it that I'm as bad as some of the others, but I wouldn't want to be singled out as one who got an amnesty when others didn't. I think all miners ought to have an amnesty and be given a chance of having their jobs back, perhaps like on probation or something. If they don't, I don't see what I'm ever going to do with my life. My mother's a pensioner, her health's not véry good, and between the two of us we've got £54 a week coming in in total that's all, and not a penny more. I'd like to be able to take her out once in a while, she's been a hardworking woman all her life and brought up her children, this ought to be the time when I could be doing something for her. But I feel it's the other way round, I'm living off her still. I think things can't possibly get any worse, but I don't see them changing.

Part II

Praying for a finish
Betty Jeffery

A very political animal
Annie Brooks

Please just ignore us
Pauline Street

Me and my blazing hate
Jean Heaton

Not the most important person in the world
Kath Sutton

Praying for a finish
Betty Jeffery

A tall red-haired woman of twenty-eight in jeans and a grey jumper, she sat at her kitchen table with her elbows on it, her chin on her clasped hands. Sometimes her green eyes had a far-away look as she talked, slowly and softly and with long pauses, almost as though not speaking till she was sure she'd got exactly the right words.

– It wasn't an easy time for anyone, and if you were mixed up in your own mind about it like I was, that didn't make it any easier, it made it a lot lot harder. You don't like to be all the time giving your own opinion, you feel you ought to stand behind your man, after all he's the one who has to decide what's best. I won't say that Keith and me had big arguments about it or things of that sort though: in fact we didn't often much talk about it. But sometimes when we'd been through to his mother's or something of that sort, I think he was looking to me for support, and he must have known sometimes he wasn't getting it. He got very depressed and down and uncertain during the strike, so it wouldn't have been much help to him if I'd thrown in my two-pennyworth. Sometimes when we'd be coming home in the car he'd go very very quiet: he wouldn't say anything to me or to our Rosalie, but I could tell it was on his mind and sometimes I thought he was going to ask me what I thought. It sounds daft to say it now: but we've never really talked about it since, so I don't know to this day properly what his feelings really were about it.

Keith and I have been married ten years, nearly eleven now, and we've just the one daughter Rosalie. We've lived in this council house since we was married: we were engaged first, then when we knew we were for definite we went ahead. Keith's lived all his life here in Red Hill, and his mam and dad live up at the top of the village in one of those council house bungalows up there. I'm from Durham myself originally, I mean Durham city, that's where I was born. When I was six I went away for a while to live with one of my aunties in the south, in Hull. My mam had gone off with another person, my dad had another lady friend, and she didn't want to look after me: so I was brought up most of my life around Hull and Goole, I went to school there. I wasn't what you'd call a very bright pupil. When I was fifteen another of my aunties had come to live here, so I came back and got a job in one of the factories in Peterlee. Then what, I did a bit of waitressing, then I was a cleaner for a time at nights in some offices, then I was in Woolworth's for a bit. I've done quite a few different things. I got married young and then we had Rosalie: I hoped we'd have some more, only we haven't been lucky yet. I'd say on the whole I was a very quiet and sort of ordinary person most of the time. I like a bit of a singsong in the club or the pub now and again, and I enjoy a good dance: but I'm the sort of person who finds it easier when I've had a drink or two first, that helps me to relax. At the moment I've got a part-time job in a dry cleaner's shop. It doesn't pay much but at least it gets me out of the house for a few hours in the morning after Rosalie's gone to school. I'd say we were all a perfectly ordinary family, on the whole not much different from anyone else, but happy.

What the future holds for us no one can be certain with things as they are at present. I know Keith doesn't want to take redundancy if they do close down Red Hill. He's only been there five years, so he wouldn't get a large sum and then he'd be out of work. I mean redundancy's only £1,000 for each year you've worked over a certain number. I should think he's got in his mind transferring to some-where else if he has to. It's funny but it's not something we've ever sat down and talked about as much of a possi-bility, not really. I think Keith's like everyone else, he's keeping his fingers crossed and hoping they'll keep Red Hill going for a few more years like they've said. They say there's enough coal in the ground there for another four or five years, and that'd give him time to sort out something else for himself if he decided he had to leave coal mining. He's not one of those who it's in the blood: you know, it's not a sort of family tradition for him like it is with a lot of men. His father was at sea in the Merchant Navy most of his life, and Keith once said he wished he'd done the same thing. I don't think he'd up and go to sea now though: he's too fond of his home comforts, I can't see him swapping anything for that.

What struck me most was I've always thought it was a very funny thing, you know, that up to the time of the strike there was never hardly any real talk at all that they might close down Red Hill. You never even heard any mention of it. I forget exactly when it was we first came to hear the rumour, but Red Hill hadn't been one of those pits with a big question mark over it right from the beginning. Perhaps if Keith had been one of those people who was always active in the Union, going to meetings and things of that sort, he'd have heard about it sooner than he did. But I think if I remember it right it was someone in one of the shops who first mentioned the idea to me, though I don't know where she'd heard about it. So then I came home and I said to Keith 'Have you heard anything about they might close down Red Hill as one of the pits that isn't economic?' He said no, he'd heard nothing about it, it was probably only a rumour. But then, a few days later, everyone in the village was talking about it: everyone you spoke to mentioned it. The first thing I thought was that the Coal Board was trying to frighten the men back to work, and that was why they were saying it. But it was only when the men did go back to work that then they found there might be possibly something in it. I hope not, I wouldn't like to think there was: it'd make a big difference to such a lot of people's lives. It'd be the end of the village as it's been up to now at least, which is a nice village to live in, with all the people very friendly.

At the start of the strike, I know no one thought it was going to last very long. I mean not a year, nothing like that. A few weeks perhaps or a month or two, then it'd be everyone back to work again as usual, with something hammered out between the Union and the Coal Board. I must have been a bit slow-witted I think, I can remember saying to Keith 'Why don't they give you the money? How much is the difference between what they're offering you and what the Union'll accept?' We were having tea at this table, and he was sitting where you're sitting. He just shook his head, he said 'No Betty love it's not as simple as that, it's not about the money.' He was reading the paper while he was eating his tea. I can always tell when he doesn't want to talk about something, and he gets ratty if I push things, so I just let it drop. I don't think I still properly know what it was the strike was about. If they said Red Hill had to be closed because it wasn't paying its way any more, that seems sad to me. But it's what you might call one of the facts of life and you can't do anything about that. Keith and I've sometimes said that if the worst came to the worst we could always go to Canada or somewhere like that. He's got an uncle there, he's more than once written to us and said there are good jobs going for someone who's good with his hands. That's always been something Keith's liked, making things: I sometimes think it might be better while Rosalie's still young to go to somewhere like Canada and let her grow up feeling it was her country and she was part of it. I don't know though; it would be a very big step to take wouldn't it? Keith and I haven't talked about it often, but it did come up once and I think the idea's still probably there in his head. I'm less of a home body than he is, I don't think it would worry me to go. Perhaps that's because I've already had the experience of living away from my home the time I was a kiddy in Hull: it's not something seems as upsetting an idea to me as it might to someone else.

But I don't expect you want me to keep going on about that: I only talk about it because I find my mind quite often wanders off in that direction. It's not something I spend a lot of time thinking about though. Now then, anyway I'll get back to the subject of the strike. Well, it was very hard, it was, that's the first thing that has to be said. Keith got no pay at all, and the Social Security people knocked £15 a week off everybody's money as well, because they counted that as the strike pay people were getting. That wasn't fair, no one was getting any strike pay: but that was the way they looked at it. I thought about trying to get a part-time job, but Keith wouldn't hear of it. He said if I earned any money they'd only take it out of our Social Security, so we'd be no better off. I didn't get this present job in the dry cleaner's till the end of the strike: during the strike I stopped here.

The thing I found most about it was how boring it was. Keith used to sit around the place doing nothing, or we had a mongrel dog and he used to take it for long walks up on the hills there at the back. He wasn't one for going off picketing or things of that sort: I think after a time he was getting very very bored and not knowing what to do with himself. He likes his fishing now and again, so he did a fair bit of that. I didn't mind because it got him out of the house, but I did start to feel he could be occupying himself more usefully. It's not something you can say to someone though. If the Union calls you out on strike you come out on strike, you have to be loyal to your mate. When I'm talking about it now, it's very hard to remember just what we did do with ourselves all day all the time. We didn't do anything very much I know that. We neither of us smoke, and we had the food parcels from the Welfare Hall and all the rest of it, and Keith went down there for his dinner a couple of days a week. He used to hang about and have a chat with some of his mates there and perhaps have a game of snooker or something, but he didn't do much else. They had a picket line at the gates of the pit, and he went and did his turn on that when he was asked. But they had no trouble here until right the very end. He didn't go off to any of the other places, Nottinghamshire or Yorkshire or anywhere. That was nothing for Keith.

People used to say to me sometimes – I remember once

when we went down for a few days to visit my auntie in Hull – and someone who was one of her neighbours she said to me 'Your husband is one of the striking miners is he?' I thought it was just an ordinary question, I didn't know she meant anything by it: I just nodded and I said 'Yes he is.' And she turned round and she said 'Well you ought to be bloody well ashamed of yourselves.' I said 'What do you mean?' She said 'Those poor bloody policemen getting knocked about like that. What they showed on the television news last night, I think it was disgraceful.' I tried to tell her my husband wasn't one of those people who'd been responsible for the fights and all the rest of it, he just stopped at home. But she wasn't having it. To her every miner spent all his time out all day looking for pits to go to where he could have a fight with the police. It's funny the ideas people get, you don't know what to say to people of that sort.

The most difficult thing for me in the strike far and away was the money, some days you didn't know where the next meal was coming from. Rosalie had some good friends at her school, and their mums used to ask her sometimes to go and have tea at their houses. If Keith had had a hot dinner at the Hall and Rosalie was going to have a hot tea at one of her friend's, I'd make do that day with perhaps a slice of toast for my dinner and maybe an egg or something for my tea. I'm not a big eater so it wasn't any great sacrifice for me. The most difficult times was the weekend and Sunday dinners. Keith likes his food: it was hard that we could sometimes only have a meat and potato pie or something of that sort, and I had to usually make it nearly all potato not meat. Or there was fish and chips from the van. The man was good, he used to see to it when he came along this street and the next one which are mostly miners' families, everyone got bigger portions than usual because he knew we were not having a lot to eat: that was his contribution if you like. People on the whole were very good. The shop keepers would let you have things and run up a bill, even though you had to say to them you didn't know when you could pay for them. Electric lightbulbs, things of that sort: they were the unexpected expenses you couldn't budget for. I think I've always been quite good with money, but there were times in the strike when say something like the iron would go wrong and would want repairing, or Rosalie would have grown out of her shoes. They're such a price these days aren't they? Even the Co-op which is about the cheapest, you can't get a decent pair of school shoes for less than what we sometimes had to live on in the strike for everything for the whole week. I'm not what you'd call a religious person, but there were times I began to feel it would be only an earthquake or something like that that they call an act of God that would get us out of the whole bloody mess.

Most of all the thing that got me down was it went on and on so long. You'd wake up on a Monday morning and you'd think 'Perhaps this week it'll come to the end, by next week they'll all be back at work and we can get on with our lives again.' That was the only way you could keep going. I remember one day after it had been going on for, oh it must have been over the six month, and Rosalie asked me how much longer it was going to be before her dad went back to work. What can you say to a child when they ask you something like that? To be truthful, it was a question I wanted to ask him myself, but I never did because I knew it would only make him go out and go off for a long walk with the dog. But many and many a day I was, I was praying: just praying for a finish.

A very political animal
Annie Brooks

Forty-five, she was small and trim in brown slacks and a light blue blouse and cardigan. Her neatly short hair was beginning to grey slightly: her dark brown eyes sparkled in the flames' reflection as she stirred up the fire.

– Do you have a nice coal fire like this in your house? Do a lot of people in the south have coal fires? Or only the ones that come from up north originally like you eh? Ah, there's nothing to beat a good coal fire is there, it's friendly isn't it? That's what I always say, I like a good coal fire, like always having someone else in the house with you all the time even when you're on your own. You've got to look after it but if you treat it proper it'll always be a good warm friend to you.

Well, Joe and me have been married twenty-three year, and we've got a boy eighteen and a girl fifteen. We're very proud of them: Gregory's got ten CSEs, and Jackie's got hers coming up this year and I think she'll do well too. Their dad's very proud of them. He says if you've got a head full of brains you can go a long way. But they're both of them nice with it if you know what I mean. They're not out to get to the top by climbing over other people. They don't want to make money out of taking advantage of people, they want to do jobs that're good and of a sort of helping kind. At the moment all Greg can get though is washing cars in a showroom at a garage and being on the petrol pumps. Still he's lucky to have that, it was only because his dad knew the man who owned it. And Jackie, she says she wants to be a teacher: only it's not going to be easy for her to get into a college, which is what she'll have to do to be a teacher. Anyway we'll see eh? To me it's nice still having them at home, I don't baby them but I'd miss either of them if they went away. Greg pays me a bit a week out of his wages for his keep, it makes him feel independent. I don't like taking money off him, but Joe says I should, it's right. Now I'm just going to have a chicken sandwich for my dinner and a cup of tea. Have you had anything to eat today yet, would you like a sandwich and all?

— I think people in the south have got no idea what life's like for people in the north you know. The south is where the money is, they live their comfortable lives and they don't give much thought to anyone else. They're very snobby most of them aren't they? I've been to London once or twice, I thought a lot of the people there were very rude and pushy. And all of them looking so sad and unhappy, and they don't talk to you much or anything. I don't think I'd be happy living down there. And they put on airs and graces a lot of them do don't they? Have you got used to living there or would you like to come back and live in the north? Perhaps one day eh?

Joe's been in Red Hill pit for twenty-eight year. Just now he's on the hydraulics, the roof supports. Before that he was a power loader. He's on about the top rate of pay almost, I don't think he'll get much higher now. He's finding all this uncertainty a very difficult time: he's forty-five, what you might call right in the middle of his life. Not old enough to retire and not young enough to start again at the bottom of something else. All of us in the village're doing everything we can to fight the idea of a closure, because there's just no need for it. There's plenty of coal still there to be got out of the ground, it'd be a terrible waste if they were to give it all up. On top of that it would be a bad day, a very very bad day, for the whole village if Red Hill was closed. The community revolves round that pit and it always has done. The village was built because of the coal mine, and if they closed down the pit they'd be closing down the village. It's like a big dark cloud over everyone these days: they're just waiting and waiting to see what's going to happen, that's all they can do. The shopkeepers, the old-age pensioners, the children, everyone, all the people who live here, they wonder every day what's going to become of it. It's almost like now they've won the strike the Coal Board wants to keep everyone down on the ground, and give them as miserable a time as they can think of to teach them a lesson for being naughty boys.

And no one knows what it is they're supposed to have done wrong. Before the strike, the Board were transferring men here from other pits that they'd closed down, telling them they were all right there was years and years of work here. Then there's the strike, and Red Hill was pretty well one hundred per cent solid. Then only towards the end of it did we first hear mention of any suggestion at all Red Hill pit might be closed down. It was on the news on the television, they happened to mention us one night as a possibility of one of the pits that was being considered for closure after the strike. Joe and me were sitting here watching it: and we looked at each other, we couldn't believe what we was hearing. And once you've had your name mentioned by the Coal Board and it's on the news it does, it gives you a sick feeling down here in your stomach. I can't describe it, it's like a hand with a finger coming out of that box and pointing at you. 'You!' Fifteen years work there was, that's what they'd said to the men who came here, they'd have work here for them for fifteen years.

And there's another thing the Board doesn't seem to care about that I don't understand. They must have been very bad managers that they should have put in all the amount of new expensive machinery to develop the pit that they did a few years back: and now they say the pit's not economic. If it isn't economic now, how was it they didn't find out it wasn't economic before they started spending all that money? And what do they mean anyway by 'uneconomic'? How much money does it cost them to build a nuclear power station? It costs millions of pounds. How do they work out when they're spending all that money, not just millions but billions on atomic energy, how much it costs to produce electricity in that way? Is that 'economic' compared with what it costs them to get out coal? Why don't they invest that money in keeping mines open, or opening new mines, and keeping people in jobs?

And there's no thought for the young ones coming along. When you were a young man Joe's age, it was your inheritance if you wanted it, to go down the pit. Only if you wanted to, mind. But the job was there, it was yours for you if you wanted it. You could look around for other things first, you could pick and choose your own future. But it wasn't the case all you had to face was unemployment. But that's all there is for most of the young people today. Our own boy Greg, he's a bright lad but what sort of a future does he have to look forward to? He could have gone in the mine like his father, and got a bit of the hard experience which you have to get underground and a knowledge of the working conditions and then he could have gone on to be Under Manager or even Manager in his time. That was a future for him, it was there if he wanted it. Only not now, he hasn't got the prospect of a future like that now. He's washing cars.

– When we were talking the other morning I was thinking after you'd gone like you said: about what ways the strike had made a difference to me as a person. And the biggest one of the lot, and I asked Joe if he thought the same and he did, was that it's made me into a very political animal. Before the strike I was just for my husband and the kiddies and my home. I never read a book, I never went in to the library, and all I ever watched on the television was all those silly quiz games and what do they call them, chat shows. I mean imagine a woman who's got to my age and if you'd asked her what books she'd read in the last few years, about the only one she'd have been able to think of was a book of mostly pictures of the Royal Wedding. That was as far as my interest went in what went on in the world.

And you know at the beginning of the strike, I didn't understand what was going on at all, I'd no idea. But as the weeks started to go by it begun to dawn on me this was something very serious. So I asked Joe if he'd explain it all to me. He was very good: he told me like what you might call an outline of things, how the strike had started and what the reason for it was. Only he said I mustn't take his word for it, I should talk about it with other women whose husbands were on strike too, and read the newspaper and watch the television news: and we all ought to try and find out as much as we could about it. And most of all he said we should make up our own minds, about whether we thought the strike was right or not. It was just round about that time that several other women of the village decided they'd get together and have a meeting to discuss it all. So we all met in one of the women's houses, and we talked and talked about it all together. I think everyone was in much the same position as I was in, we'd none of us really thought much about things seriously. One of them had brought a book, a history of the Durham miners: a very good book, I've got it, you can borrow it if you like. It shows you how the mining industry in this area has gone down and down over the years like: but it also tells you the whole history of the coalfield, and gives you an idea what a fine proud tradition coal miners have.

The thing that came over clearest to me was how all the way through, every little advantage or good thing the miners got, it was always the Union that got it for them. It wasn't the bosses who gave it them: the bosses gave nothing and they usually opposed flat out what it was the men wanted. They had some very great miners' Union leaders in those past days, and there was always this great tradition in the industry that miners stuck together. I don't think there's another union in the country that's got a history a patch on anything like that of the miners. That's why there's all the bitterness now about this breakaway union, the UDM, the Union of Democratic Mineworkers. 'Democratic Mineworkers'! It makes you laugh: it's something that's been set up with financial help from the Coal Board and the Government and money from a lot of right-wing politicians. All it is is just to try and cause a split in the NUM. It hasn't got any independence, any history, and not a single self-respecting mining Union man who's anything to do with it. They say those letters UDM, they really stand for 'Under Direct Management' by the Coal Board. Daft as muck they must be those men, to let themselves be used like that.

Well I get a bit carried away don't I? But I feel so strong about it. Anyway what was I telling you, yes about the meeting that we women had. We decided we'd form a Women's Support Group in the village, and I think Red Hill were one of the first. The idea was we wanted to let the Coal Board and the Government see we were right behind the men, and we wanted to be a force to be reckoned with as well as the menfolk. They couldn't say the only people active in the strike were just the greedy ones wanting money. There was a principle in it, the principle that we wanted to save jobs, not have our men put out of work and thrown on the dole. And we wanted to have a future for our communities where we lived and for our children.

I was the one chosen to be the head of the group in this area. But we had it all on a very informal basis: we decided right at the start we weren't going to get bogged down with committee meetings and keeping notes and minutes and all things of that sort. We were much more interested to do something practical to help. The most obvious thing to start with was to try and collect money that'd provide food and clothing for the families that were going short. They were suffering, believe me. So we went around, we went in the clubs and pubs with collecting boxes, we went in the shops and asked them if they would donate things, we went everywhere. People were really marvellous about it, everyone was: I know it sounds funny but it was true, one night I went in the local Conservative Club rattling my tin and saying 'Money for the striking miners' – would you

believe it, there was no hesitation, for not even a minute.
All round the room people put their hands in their pockets
and their handbags, and I collected a really big sum of
money that night.

Then of course it started to get in the newspapers and
on the telly, about the women's Support Groups, and it
really took off. People began sending us money from all
over the country, and asking us to send speakers to various
places to tell them what was going on. We all went wherever we could, one to this place, someone else to another,
women who'd never in our lives done anything like it
before. It didn't half give you a funny feeling at first. If
you'd told me ten years ago or even five years ago that I'd
ever stand up on a stage in front of a packed hall and speak
to an audience of two hundred people, I'd have said not
me, I couldn't do it, it wouldn't be possible. But I found
I wasn't even hardly frightened. It was because I believed
in what we were doing, and thought people weren't being
told the full truth, the half truth, or sometimes not even
any of the truth about our case and what was really going
on.

It was the only thing we could do, try to put our side of
the case. Most people in the country only saw the television, the pushing and the shoving on the picket lines, the
police getting squashed and having bricks thrown at them.
They didn't see what I saw, not once but dozens and
dozens of times – brave women scratching meals together
for their families, houses where they couldn't afford to
light the fire except at weekends, women going around in
their very oldest clothes with no hope of any new ones,
because if there was any money at all it all had to go on
feeding their families. And they didn't know what I knew
either, which was that Government was out to smash the
Union. I'm not a member of the NUM, I couldn't be
because I'm a woman. But I could see what it told you in
that book about the Union's history and that the Government had had enough of it and was going to try to crush
them.

They had their leader Arthur Scargill, and he was one of the great leaders in the tradition of all the other miners' leaders whose names are in the book. He might have made a few mistakes but he's only human: I think he's one of the greatest men the Union've ever had. Long before the strike started he said the National Coal Board had a hit list of the pits they were going to close, and they were trying to keep it secret because they knew how much trouble there'd be if it was ever published. And what did they say? Did they say what was the truth, that yes they did have a list and they were keeping it secret? No they damn well didn't: they said he was talking rubbish, there wasn't no list, he was just a troublemaker and no one should listen to him. And then what do we find out in the end? We find out that what he said was the absolute truth. They had a hit list, they have a hit list, and they daren't tell anyone about it or say its details.

The other thing Arthur Scargill said was this Government was determined on bringing down the National Union of Mineworkers, and they wouldn't rest until they'd done it. Oh no the Government said, that wasn't true, it was all lies. Well it wasn't all lies, it was all true. There's not a thing Scargill has ever said that anyone's ever been able to point to and say 'There you are, he was lying.' If they want to prove to people Scargill isn't what he says he is, a leader of the miners with only their interests at heart, well go on then let them prove it. But they don't: they can't. But he can prove what he said about the Board and the Government is right, every damn word of it.

This Government, all they care about and all they've ever cared about is the rich man's pocket, and how more money can be put into it. If you look at the whole picture in this country, what you see is that the people in the City of London, the bankers and the stockbrokers and the people like that who deal in money – they're the ones who're making more and more money every day. They have their big houses and their flashy cars, they wine and dine themselves in expensive restaurants, they have their children at expensive schools. Half of them live in big houses of their own where half a dozen of the likes of us and our families could fit in. But all they think about is how they can fiddle their taxes, how they can pay less tax, and how they can set up crooked companies so they can make even bigger profits.

I'm not a communist, I wouldn't even call myself a proper socialist: I'm too selfish in my outlook. I haven't reached the stage where I feel everything should be for the good of the state, I want to keep a few things of our own for the good of my family. But it was talking to people, and listening to people and reading books out of the library, that helped me see the sort of society we've got in this country today, and how it's an unfair one. Those who've got riches find it easier to make more riches: while those who've only got what they can get by working manually, whose only assets are in their hands, they're the ones who never get far in life. Her on the box, she comes on and lectures us all about what she calls 'Victorian values' and how we ought to get back to those days of Christianity and morality and family life. Well she's a fine one to talk: but I'm not being cruel and just talking about those two deadbeats she's got as her own children. I'm talking about her and her husband's rich business friends, who go and make a few thousand pounds at their offices in the City of London before dinner, then go off to a club for eating and drinking and spend their afternoons on the golf course. And at night nightclubs and gambling clubs and any other way they can think of as to how to spend all the money that they've got. I've heard it said, and I believe it, that what one of those City gentlemen in his flash suit makes in a week is more than everyone in this street outside here earns in a year. I think people like that ought to be ashamed of themselves: but they look down on the likes of us because they don't think we're clever. Well all right, not in their terms we're not clever. But in their hearts I hope they must know they're rotten people.

– It did a lot for Joe and me's marriage did the strike: everything it did was good. We'd sometimes hardly saw each other for twenty-four hours on end: he'd be coming in that door from his turn on the picket line just as I was going off out to a meeting. All we'd have time for was 'Hello' and that was it. He didn't have to tell me he was proud of what I was doing, I could see it in the way he looked at me. I was always up in the clouds when I came back from a meeting or something, and I'd start rattling away at him and telling him all about it. And he'd sit and listen and talk with me about it, it was a whole new interest in life for both of us. One day he gave me a smile and he said sometimes he felt he ought to write a post card that said 'Dear Mr Scargill, When this is all over, please can I have my wife back?' The whole business made me much more of a thinking person: I could never go back to being like I was before. We see something on the TV news now, and if it's something political we wait till it's over and then we talk about it, discuss it between ourselves, Joe puts his view about it and I put mine. It's made our life together a lot more interesting, we both feel we're part of each other's lives much more. We don't like a lot of what's going on in the country, we think nearly everything those Tories do is downright disgusting. But at least we talk about it and decide between us why we don't agree with it. If it's a subject we don't know enough about, I'll go to the library next day to see if they've got a book about it that'll tell us more. It might be the famine in Ethiopia say, or what's happening in Afghanistan, or something of that sort. Now I feel I'm much better informed about these things it helps me enjoy life more.

Mind you it's easier for me though. Poor Joe, he doesn't know what's going to happen at the pit, whether this time next year he's going to have a job or whether he isn't. He says sometimes he feels he can hardly dare breathe. It's a horrible thing to see a man who's had a hard-working life in that sort of a situation where he feels he can't do nothing himself to alter it. A good man who's provided for his family and tried to give them some decent values. That sort of man's the salt of the earth: I don't think the present Government of this country should be allowed to get away with what they're doing to men like him. But then we're not public figures, we're only unknown people.

Even if it came at the next election that the Tories were beat and I hope to God they are – but even if it came to that, I don't think afterwards they should be allowed to forget what they've done and get away with it. The usual thing is someone who's been a Prime Minister, when they come to the end of their time they're put up to the House of Lords. Well if that Thatcher woman is ever made Lady something or other, I don't think it ought to be allowed. It's supposed to be a mark of gratitude by the nation. In her case there's nothing the ordinary people of this country and their children have got anything to be grateful to her for at all. All she's given us is bitterness, division and strife and unhappiness and humiliation, loss of pride in ourselves and loss of our way of life. That should be remembered for ever, and when the time comes she shouldn't be thanked for it, she ought to be called to account for it. That's my view of her.

Please just ignore us
Pauline Street

– Oh nothing like the strike time had ever happened to me before in the whole of my life. It changed me completely. I was very quiet before, I wouldn't say boo to a goose. I'd scarcely talk to anybody, I certainly wouldn't have been able to sit here like this and talk to you, have someone I didn't know in my house. I'd be polite if I met you, but I'd let you do all the talking, I wouldn't be saying anything. The strike changed it all. It made me stronger and have a lot more confidence in myself and my own opinions. for all the dreadful things that happened and all the terrible hard time we went through, there were some things about it that I did, I thoroughly enjoyed. It was because I was active, I was joining in and I felt I was taking part. Even though I had three kiddies and I was pregnant as well, I used to wonder to myself sometimes whatever I'd done with my time before. Down at the Hall three days a week, dishing up dinners for three hundred people, clearing up and doing the washing-up afterwards – I mean you'd think if you were six months pregnant you'd feel exhausted at the end of a day of that wouldn't you? But I didn't, I used to come home feeling all bubbly inside and with my eyes shining. I always got back here in time for the bairns coming home from school, then I was ready to give them their teas and do the washing and get Alf's meal for when he came in. It ought to sound wrong to say being in the miners' wives' Support Group was terrific, and now the strike's over I look back and think it was one of the best times I had in my life, shouldn't it? Does it make me sound daft?

With her eleven-month energetic baby girl climbing all over her, as she laughed and reminisced she swung her from her lap to the floor, picked her up again, held her up in the air

*and cooed at her. Her long golden hair tumbled round her
face as she talked, unresponsive to head shakes and hand
flicks attempting to keep it in order. Somehow as well she
held a mug of coffee and some biscuits, sipping and nibbling
and giving morsels to her baby.*

– The best description of me would be I'm a housewife
and a mum. I'm thirty, and this one's my fourth one and
my last one, aren't you treasure, eh? All girls, the eldest's
ten, the others're eight and six: two of them take after me
and two of them after Alf. They're all treasures and this
one's the biggest treasure of all eh?

I can tell you it was bloody hard, I shouldn't say that
should I, I'll say it was very hard in the strike trying to
feed two grown-ups and three kids, all on £40-odd a week.
But I had a good mam and so did Alf: coal mining's in both
our families, both our fathers was miners all their lives,
and they helped us out because they knew what it was like.
But it was very very hard, and sometimes I did get very
down about it.

I got very angry sometimes too, that was my other main
feeling. Is it all right if I use the word 'scab'? That was
what we called them, the scabs: and they were the ones, I
could honestly have killed them. The ones over at Waddell
Moor, some of them live just the other side of those fields
over on that council estate. Sometimes I felt I could march
over there on my own and ask their wives weren't they
ashamed of their men, how could they let them go on
doing what they were doing? I didn't go on the picketing
because I didn't want to run the risk of getting knocked
about when I was pregnant. But I would have gone on a
demonstration if there'd been one on that estate against
those people over there.

Alf got pushed about on the picket line but that was all,
he wasn't one of the ones who got into trouble. I had to
laugh sometimes: I mean it wasn't really funny but he came
home one day from picketing and he was bare to the waist.
I asked him what had happened to his T-shirt and he said

a copper had ripped it off his back just like that. Mostly though he spent most of his time out on the coal tips picking up coal.

Anyhow: down at the Hall where we were doing the feeding, we made sure that every man who wanted it got at very least two hot meals a week: usually pie and peas and gravy, or potatoes and meat. We got a terrific lot of help from the shops in the village, they were marvellous: they gave us vegetables, or let us buy pies cheap, that sort of thing. We paid them as much as we could afford from the money we'd collected, but there wasn't a single time when they didn't ask us how many we were going to feed that day, and made it up so we'd have enough. I think some of the wives in the village could have given us more help with the serving than they did, after all it was their husbands came and helped with the eating of the food. But quite a few didn't.

– These women who went round speaking at meetings like Annie, I thought it was terrific. I think it's good that ordinary people should tell other ordinary people about the strike. The way it was put over on the television and in the papers, we was all irresponsible people who only wanted to have a punch-up with the police if it was the men, or stand on street corners shouting if it was the women. But it wasn't like that everywhere or often: in fact round here it was never like that, except right at the end. We weren't asking for the world, all we wanted was security for our husbands' jobs.

I think Red Hill is a good village to live, I've lived here all my life and so's Alf. I don't mean to look at, I can't see it would ever be in a picture book of photographs of beautiful England. There's lots of people would look at it and to them it'd just be a dark and dreary place, with nothing different to it from a hundred other pit villages. They'd say to themselves well what'd be lost if this village didn't have its pit no longer? Well, me, I'd answer that by saying what would be lost would be the heart and soul of all the people who live in it, and who've lived here for not just our generation or our parents' but from even before that.

All we want is our men's jobs, and to be able to get on with our own lives, and have enough money for us and our kids to live on, that's all we ask. We don't want no big enormous sports centres or leisure complexities, or posh parks or swimming baths: we like it here like it is. I mean obviously we like good things for the children, or for them to do in the evenings. But if you've lived here all your life, this is your home, this is where you belong. When I go even to Peterlee on the bus shopping, I'm glad to come back here at the end of the afternoon: I wouldn't want to live there, I don't think the place has got any character to it at all. It's too modern for me: I'm a plain old-fashioned lass I am, and I'm happy to think when I'm walking down that street there that's where my mam and dad walked, and their mam and dads in their day before them.

It wouldn't suit everyone, I know. My sister, she doesn't feel like that: when she got married she went through to live in Newcastle. She likes the big city life, she said she didn't care if she never saw Red Hill again in all her life. She and me are totally different in every way. She married someone who is on the buses: and I know he works very hard, but we did, we fell out very badly with them in the strike. They got it all off the telly, they were always telling us why did we listen to Arthur Scargill and what an evil wicked man he was. One day I said to Billy my brother-in-law, I said 'From what you're always saying about your working conditions, the way they mess you about, put men off and then take new ones on again a few weeks later for lower wages, it sounds to me you could do with someone like Arthur Scargill to lead you.' But Billy works for a private company who're very strong against the unions, and his bosses are taking advantage of him and his mates – and yet he's against the unions. You can't understand how some people's minds work can you?

But my sister in the strike, she was even worse. When

we went there she used to get me in the kitchen and say 'Stop being so bloody stupid Pauline, get your Alfie to go back to work and behave like a grown-up. You've got your children to think of, this isn't all a laugh and a joke.' That was because I didn't want us to have rows with them in their house, I always used to laugh and smile and say we'd brought the children to see them and we'd come to see their children, we hadn't all come to have an argument. My sister is older than me, she's always thought I haven't any brains. We're different every way you can think of. Their house is always neat and tidy: you'd never see it look anything like this, toys all over the floor so you can hardly walk without breaking your ankle. At the end of the day her kiddies have to put every single one of their toys away on the shelves or in a cupboard. It's not a house where they give you a feeling they enjoy children.

I think it was very sad there was a lot of families like ours where the strike caused a big division between them. I used to tell my sister she ought to remember our dad, whose side was she on? She said that wasn't a fair thing to say: I suppose it wasn't, really. He's had four strokes and he can't talk now. But I know whose side he would be on if he could, he'd be on the side of the miners. He was a miner himself all his life, and you don't change your allegiance. I could see from the way he looked at me when I was telling him about going down to the Welfare Hall to help with the dinners, or about Alfie losing his shirt on the picket line. He'd smile and nod his head, and he wouldn't have done that if he hadn't been with us in what we were doing. So well we don't go to Newcastle much now: I think it's going to be a long time for a lot of people before they get over what happened in the strike.

Those of us who were in it and for it, I sometimes think we're never going to get over it. I know Alfie would, and I certainly would, I'd still go all through it all again if it was necessary. I'm very proud of my husband and the fact he didn't go back to work until the Union said. And I'm proud of our family, our parents and our children, who all played their part. They were all affected. Our two eldest girls'd sometimes come back from school and they'd say so-and-so's father was scabbing. They used that word, they said they'd been shouting it in the playground. But I don't hold with that, and I told them I didn't. I said the best thing was just not to speak to the children at all. Only you can't help it, you do feel proud if your children are telling you they're supporting their father and all the striking miners, even when it means they're having to go without things themselves.

I said I'd go through it all again, and I would. Only I don't think there'll be an again. To be honest about it I think it's all over now. The Coal Board can do as they want now, and nothing'll stop them. They could even close Red Hill if they wanted, though we hope to God they won't. The only thing Thatcher didn't get that she wanted was Arthur Scargill's head on a plate. That's one thing she'll never have: mining people are very very loyal to him because he was a real leader to them. He speaks the truth, he says exactly how things are, he doesn't hold out false promises and he's a very responsible sort of person. He was pushed into this strike, he had no choice. Sometimes it seemed as though the whole country was against him, there wasn't anyone who'd say a good word in support of him in the newspapers or on the telly. But his own people always had good words for him: they knew he was their champion and to them he still is.

– I was saying yesterday about sometimes enjoying the strike. But don't get me wrong about it, there was a lot of suffering, for everyone, no mistake about that. Over a year after it most of us is still paying off debts and will be for a long time. We've got a decent sympathetic local council, they've not pushed us for rents, and everybody else has been reasonable when it came to electricity bills and other household things. But nobody's taking advantage of it, one way or another everybody's going to pay off their debts however long it takes.

I'll tell you something made me laugh: well it didn't but it does now. One time when the strike was on I got a little part-time job: for a month I went cleaning at one of the schools where the regular cleaner was sick and couldn't go in. Alf stayed at home and looked after the children, so we'd sort of changed round: he did the housework, the dishes and the hoovering and the rest of it, and I brought home the money. It wasn't much, £25 a week. The first week or so was all right, and I used to get home about two o'clock. As soon as I did, he was on the couch there with his feet up, reading the paper. After a bit I said to him one day 'I didn't do that when you used to come home after work, Alf.' He said to me 'What d'you mean, what is it you want then, d'you want for me to make you a cup of tea?' I said no it wasn't that: doing the house was my job when he was working, so why shouldn't it be his job when I was working? It was him who was running the house now, so he ought to get the children's tea and put them to bed, not just pack up and leave it to me when I came in. We had quite a bit of a row about it. Anyway in the end he saw it and agreed: and after that we used to make a joke about it, when I came home he used to be waiting for me with an apron on. I wouldn't risk letting him go as far as trying to bake a cake, but he was very good. The kids thought it was a real laugh their dad should be running around dressed up like that. I'm not a women's libber or anything though: I'd say I'm sort of in the middle. But I am reading about women's rights and all things like that, and taking a big interest in the subject. That's something I'd give as an example to you of how I've changed: before the strike I'd never have given it a thought.

We tried our best to keep up a laugh and a joke in front of the children all the time, but it wasn't always easy to do. The very hardest of all was at Christmas, when there was no money in the house at all and it didn't look like the kids were any of them going to . . . I mean not like it'd been previous times at Christmas . . . we really really didn't know how we were going to give them any presents

. . . and . . . and we told them and they said it was all
right, they understood and it was all right, we mustn't
worry about . . . I'm sorry, please just ignore us, I still get
all choked up when I talk about it. They all said . . . they
all said Christmas didn't matter, they didn't mind about
having no presents from us like they usually had. You feel
awful about it, you feel you've let them down really bad
. . . I'm sorry, I shall be all right in a minute. If anyone
were to see me they'd think I was daft, they would, they'd
think I'd gone mad. 'Pauline's always the one who's laughing and joking about.' Let's go on, honestly really I'm all
right. I think I wasn't expecting to be talking about it, but
don't look at us, go on asking me questions, it's good for
me to talk about it, I never have, much.

Oh but in the end it was funny, I have to laugh about it
because what saved us was Bunty. That's her there, she's
Bunty, our dog. Just one week before Christmas she had
three pups, really beautiful they were. We said anyone
who wanted them could have them but a man came over,
a farmer from Browley, and he said he'd take all three
when they were big enough in the New Year, and he gave
us £20 for them there and then. So we were able to say to
the kids that Bunty'd given them their Christmas presents
that year, which she had.

– I wish I knew what was going to happen but if you think
about the future you can only say you don't know, there's
nobody knows what's going to happen. I've got the feeling
in my own mind they're after us, you feel they're really
going to try and punish us for going on strike. I don't think
that horrible MacGregor man will have any mercy on
anyone. I suppose that's why Mrs Thatcher chose him,
because he was a man after her own heart. There's those
who say she hasn't got any heart either: what did she call
herself, the Iron Woman? She knows herself better than
anyone. Solid iron outside and not a thought for anyone
else. They always say don't they women are softer than
men, but she isn't, she hasn't ever been. I'm not political

because I've got no ideas about it and I don't understand it. I understand Labour a bit more than I do the Conservatives, but that's because I was brought up in a house where we always voted Labour.

I don't really care which sort of Government we have so long as it's a decent and caring one. You want your children when they grow up in the world to be honest and decent and caring, and you look to the country's leaders to set the example. But this lot we've got now, how can anyone point to them, to their children and say one day they hope they'll grow up like that? When she comes on the television now I can't bear to look at her, I get up and go out of the room, make a cup of tea or something.

I've enjoyed talking, talking's something I enjoy a lot: I don't get the chance as much as I did during the strike. As things are I'm a bit frightened about what's going to happen in the future here at Red Hill, all this talk of they might close the pit. We've not made any plans, Alf and me, but whatever it is we'll face it. When I was saying to you the strike had made me stronger and given me more confidence in myself, that was another way I meant it. It made me that from now on I wasn't just going to go along behind Alf through life, leaving everything to him. I've got a contribution to make to life too, my own opinions and my strength to add in with his. There was a smashing song one of the women wrote we used to sing at our meetings: that said it all, every word of it. I can't remember it now but it was wonderful, it became a sort of hymn for us. It was great, it meant such a lot to us it did. 'Here we go, for the women of the working class.'

Me and my blazing hate
Jean Heaton

A tall and heavily built dark-haired woman in her early thirties, she was rarely able at first to sit still for more than a few minutes at a time while she talked. She preferred to prowl round and round in her small sitting room in the terraced house, anger sparkling off her in all directions, her voice fiercely harsh with her feelings. She chain-smoked.

– He says it'll burn me up in flames one day, my husband does, me and my blazing hate. He says it can't be kept up for ever, you've got to forgive and forget. I'll never forget, that's one thing that's sure: and I'll never forgive neither, at least I can't see myself doing. The Coal Board's turned my husband, who all his life's been an honest upright working man, into a criminal. They've made him someone with a conviction, and a criminal record for it. And as well as that they've made him into someone who because of it'll never again in his whole life get a decent job. He did nothing wrong in the first place: but they won't relent and give him his job back. So neither will I relent either. Those people, the Coal Board, Ian MacGregor, Maggie Thatcher, the Tories – I hate every one of them and I'll hate them till my dying day for what they've done to my husband. He can forgive them if he likes, and if he does he's a better person and a better Christian than I am. To me they're the biggest bastards who ever walked the face of the earth, and every morning when I get up I curse them and I curse them every night when I go to bed.

You wouldn't think it to hear me now but I was a very quiet person before. I looked after the house and my husband and my children, some days I went to the shops, then I came back and did the housework and cooked for them and kept the house neat and tidy and clean. I've a boy of nine, that's Barry, and a girl of eleven, Janine. Just a housewife, that's all I ever was was a housewife, right from when I left school when I was fifteen. Now I'm thirty-two I suppose I'm just a housewife still to look at me from the outside. But inside I'm a very angry person, and I shall stay angry until we've got rid of this rotten Government and the rotten system it makes us live under. If they'd give my husband his job back and his rights as a human being that's all I ask, that'd be enough for me. I'd still never forget what they'd done, but I might forgive. But not until that day comes, no.

It's hard to explain, I'm not a good talker. For over a year now my husband's been on the dole. His whole life before that, he'd worked every day of his life. In all the time I've known him he never had more than two days off work once when he'd got a bad cold. That's in fifteen years. But hard work and loyalty doesn't get you anywhere does it if your employers are the Coal Board. I can't say words you'd think fit to print about them. He worked seven years underground, then he had an accident so after that they put him as a driver on one of their maintenance trucks.

What happened was the strike had been going six months and they nailed him. He's always been active in the Union, and they knew him: so they picked him off, he was one of the ones who'd not been an easy man for them to deal with. They took the opportunity to get rid of him and a few others, and now they won't let any of them back. He was supposed to have driven his van at somebody over at Waddell Moor when there was a fuss there one morning. They said he deliberately nearly ran someone down. When you meet Ted you'll find he's a very quiet person, you see if you think he's the sort of man who'd try and do that. The police stopped his van and pulled him out: when they charged him, they told him he was going to get three months in Durham Gaol: and in the end all he got was a fine. But he was told there was another charge, of causing an affray, which would lie on the books. Then the week before Christmas he got the letter from the Coal Board: it said as he'd been convicted, he wasn't working for them anymore because the offence was on Coal Board property. At Waddell Moor pit gates there's a curve in the road like that, and that's where it happened, it wasn't anywhere near on Coal Board property. Fifteen years he's worked for them, he's been to the Union to see if they can help I don't know how many times, but he can't get back. He's not the only man prominent in the Union they've got rid of and won't take back: if you was a Union man they take any excuse they can now to be shot of you. They use Ted and people like him as an example to try and frighten the others.

It's funny, I had a feeling for quite a bit beforehand they were after him and something was going to happen. Only about a week before the police came knocking on this front door here and asked where he was. I knew where he was, he'd gone to a Union meeting over near Easington, but I didn't see it had anything to do with them, so I said he was out. There was this big police sergeant and he said to me 'When he comes back tell him we've been here asking for him. There's been some incidents at Durnston and two people there've said they identified him.' I said 'Don't be bloody ridiculous;' I said, 'He's nowhere near Durnston this morning.' The sergeant looked at me and he said 'I thought you just said you didn't know where he is.' I said 'I don't know where he is, but I do know he's not gone anywhere near Durnston.'

After they'd gone, it gave me a nasty feeling, an inkling they were trying to pin something on him. When he came back I told him about it and said he'd better be careful. It shows you how honest he is, Ted said 'Don't be daft, police don't go around trying to pin things on people, I wasn't nowhere near Durnston, I was at Easington, so it couldn't have been me.' I said I knew it and he knew it, but he'd better take it as a warning. He said he thought that was probably all what it was, they were just trying to scare him.

But they got him in the end, they found something: the threatening driving thing. From now on, if I ever saw a policeman now I wouldn't give him the time of day. If someone stuck a knife in a policeman out there on that pavement outside the front door, as far as I'm concerned I'd leave him there and let him bleed to death. It's a shocking thing I know that someone should be talking like that about the police. I've never liked them much and I've never been in trouble with them, but I did have respect for them, I thought they could be mistaken if you like now and again, but I honestly didn't know how far they would go. But the day we went to court, there was two of them actually stood up one after the other, and they gave exactly the same evidence word for word about what they said Ted had done, how he'd driven his vehicle deliberately at somebody. One trouble was he didn't have a decent barrister, the man he'd got was not sympathetic to the striking miners at all, so he didn't question them properly. One of the policemen said he saw the incident from one side of the street, how Ted's lorry narrowly missed going over this man's foot and he had to jump out of the way: then the other one said he saw it from the other side of the street, exactly the same thing. How that could be I don't know, because it was a big lorry: if you're on this side you can see what happens on this side, but if you're on the other side you can't see what's happening this side at all.

I think the police have done themselves a lot of harm: they have all round here anyway, that's true and I don't think you'd find many who'd tell you different. One night when there was a bit of trouble up at the pit gates – well I say trouble, just someone had got in and pinched a bit of coal and they were after him – the police chased this man right down these backs outside here, and right into someone's backyard at nine o'clock at night. So Andy who lives at number 17, he'll tell you about it himself, he went out of his back door and he saw these five policemen all on top of this one man. He said to them 'Heh, this is my house, this is my backyard, what d'you think you're doing?' And one of them actually said to him 'Well if it's your house, you get back inside it or you'll get the effing same.' In his own backyard, in this day and age! To me, that's thugs, that's all they are. Ready to do just whatever they're told and they'll turn on their own class and kick them and beat them as soon as look at them.

Oh yes I can tell you, I'm full of hate. Some nights I can't sleep for sheer hate.

– I don't think anyone whose husband was active in the strike – I mean active in the Union, I'm not talking about demonstrating on the picket lines – no one can ever be the same afterwards. What happened at Red Hill was there was a good strong feeling of solidarity, everybody was behind the Union. There wasn't no fights outside the gates or things of that sort, because there wasn't a man who worked there who tried to go back. They were absolutely solid until right at the very very end. So at Red Hill you had a good Union pit. And there were good relations between the management and the men, there always had been there. But the Coal Board thought that if they could get a split between the workers, some wanting to go back and others not, they would be laughing, they'd weaken the Union's strength. So they tried, and they tried hard: but whatever they offered in the way of cash and special bonuses, there wasn't a crack anywhere. All the time, everyone was completely solid behind the Union. So it's obvious now isn't it why they've suddenly decided to consider closing the whole pit? There was never any talk of it before, it was a pit they said had got a lot of coal in it, they transferred men from other pits they'd closed and told them they'd got security here. Now they've suddenly turned round and started saying it's uneconomic. Have you seen that book they did at the University, about how the Board makes a pit sound as though it's losing money, using these figures and those figures but not the other figures that aren't convenient? And what's at the bottom of it isn't whether the pit's economic or not, it's trying to shut down a pit where the Union's solid and strong. Well they've not succeeded, and God willing they're not going to succeed at Red Hill. The feelings are too strong: it's a good pit, and one which has got plenty of coal in it for a good few years yet.

Some people might tell you they enjoyed the strike, others'd say they were near breaking point with being short and they don't know how they survived it. I wouldn't be one of those who said I enjoyed it, most of the time I was too frightened. I was frightened about what they was going to try and do to Ted, it was as simple as that. I never told him at the time how frightened I was, but in the end it turned out that I was right: I knew he'd be one on their list as the sort of Union activist they were determined to get rid of. After he'd been arrested the court gave him bail conditions which said that he couldn't go out far anywhere at any time, specially not at night: he had to be in the house here at seven o'clock, and he wasn't to even put his nose outside the front door to go and get a packet of cigarettes till nine the next morning. That was to stop him doing his Union work, that was the point to that.

One night we heard there was some coal in the stock yard, it'd been brought in in secret by lorries and dumped there, and they were going to take it away again the next day. I'm not sure what the idea was, I think it was something they were trying to set up for the television, to give the impression there was still some coal being produced from the pit. This was the November, the weather was very very cold. Anyway word got round this coal was there, so quite a lot of people thought they'd go and help themselves to a bit of it.

Ted said he'd borrow a car and take it round the back of the pit where the coal was, then some of the men were going to climb over the fence and fill up a few sacks for themselves and their families. I was petrified: I knew if anything went wrong and the police did happen to catch them it would be prison for Ted. So I went across to see Sandra over the road and one or two of the other wives and I told Ted he wasn't to go. We'd decided we'd go first, the women. I think we felt if there was any danger, the police would be less likely to rough women up than they would men. We all remembered what had happened down the back here with the man they'd chased into Andy's. So we got some plastic shopping bags and six of us went off: it was pitch dark and I think every one of us was frightened out of our wits. Somebody had pulled off one or two of the planks in the fence, so there was a gap we could get through. My heart was banging against my ribs, I thought everyone round the whole village would hear it. It was the first time in my life I'd gone to steal a single thing, and I was terrified about it. But anyway we got the coal, I think we had about two shopping bags full each. I came in through that back door, I put them down on the hearth there and I said to Ted and the children 'There you are, that was stolen for you with love.' And oh it did, it burned real lovely.

– Because he's been sacked and can't go and have his job back, Ted has lost any chance of redundancy money, so what there is in life for us now neither of us knows. I think it's only anger keeps me going: I do believe there's still some justice in this country, and if in the end we get a different government, it'll be one that gives the miners a fair deal. A hundred years or more they've provided this country with its life blood, and I don't think people will forever go on letting the Government spit on them and tell them they're troublemakers and should be treated like naughty schoolboys. I think when people realise what's been going on and what's being done to the working people here, someone is bound to come along and say 'Stop it, that's enough of that.'

The only man who's said it to the Government so far is Arthur Scargill: in my eyes he's a king of a man. He brought the miners to see what the Coal Board was trying to do with them, and they backed him on it for a full year. You only need to think about that to realise what he means to them. I've never talked to no one who would ever say they felt he'd let them down. Even when it came to the vote for going back, he accepted the vote of the other people on the Executive with him. He didn't agree with it, but he accepted it. He's a true man and someone that people can look up to. It's a pity that the country hasn't got more like him, not just the miners. Arthur Scargill is for the working man, and I hope one day he gets to be the head of the Labour movement. I don't call myself a political person, I've never understood the ins and outs of it all: but I think you'd have to go a long way before you found anyone like him.

The other thing I'd like to say is that I don't think we ever got a fair deal from the media. When you think who owns the press I don't suppose that's very surprising: but it turns me up now when you hear people talking about our 'free press'. It's only free for you if you're a millionaire ten times over and you put over the Government's point of view for them. Through the strike we had a lot of journalists here asking us things: and they tried to give us the impression all they wanted was the facts. But they didn't, they was all doing jobs they'd been told to do. They used to go to meetings every few days up at the Coal Board headquarters up here, where they were given handouts. All they reported was from the Coal Board's point of view: I never read a word anywhere that put over anything different. You don't expect to have something so one hundred per cent one-sided, you do expect a bit of fairness in reporting.

And television, well nobody who wasn't here knows how bad that was, and how they only showed what they were allowed to show. There's a friend of my sister's, he works for a commercial television company: he says so many things were cut out and not shown on the news it was almost at the point where a lot of them were thinking of going on strike themselves. Anything that showed the police in a bad light was forbidden: but anything that showed miners as a rowdy shouting mob, that was all right. He told us of one instance where there'd been some trouble on a picket line at one particular pit, and the news editor or whoever he was came in and said 'These pictures are no good, it doesn't look like anything's happening at all, haven't you anything better?' They said they hadn't, because nothing much had happened. So he told them to put in some film they'd taken six weeks beforehand, of a different incident at a different pit, and put it in to go with this story. He said to them 'People won't know the difference and it'll ginger it up a bit.'

And I think one other point to get over is that in the strike and all the things that went on, a lot of our children saw those things and it's going to affect the way they grow up. They don't look on the police as nice kind friendly people at all. Our two, they've seen and heard some police behaviour on their own bus taking them to school. One day it went past some policemen standing in a line, and all the kids shouted out of the window at them like kids do. A police van came after them and made the bus stop, and four policemen jumped on the bus and started shouting 'Stand up the little bastards who were shouting at us back there, come on, let's see how brave you are now.' I don't think any child is going to grow up with liking policemen if they behave in that sort of fashion. All they're after doing is trying to frighten kids: they might succeed, but they won't ever get them to like them. And other things our two know is they've seen and heard what happened to their own father, how evidence was made up against him: and they know the boy in their class who's the son of Andy, the man whose backyard they came running into and beating that man in. I think this is very serious for the future, and I think the police should be aware of it.

The strike's still all very real to me. I live with the effects of it on Ted and my family every day. Sometimes I can talk calmly about it, not like I was the first time. But inside my feelings are still just the same, I'm full of hate. A hating person, that's not a very nice thing to say you've become is it?

Not the most important person in the world
Kath Sutton

She talked in her firm quiet voice in her office, gently turning herself from side to side in the high-backed swivel chair behind her desk. Area Co-ordinator of the Women's Support Groups. During the first quarter of an hour the phone rang so many times eventually she asked the switchboard operator for a short period of respite without interruptions.

– I think most of the women involved in the Support Groups at the time of the strike will tell you that it was a kind of turning point of their lives, that they'll never be the same again now afterwards. I'm no different from the rest of them, except perhaps that I had already been involved in a few community things. But not of that kind: I was a sort of generalised do-gooder, Girl Guides and that sort of thing. I wouldn't say I was political in any way at all, though I did seem to have a sense of the importance of things. I remember for instance when I was at school at fourteen I got up a petition in support of the nurses in their pay dispute. I didn't know any nurses but it just seemed to me they were in the right, so I got as many of the other girls in the school as I could to sign a petition to the Health Minister about it. I'd say I was well-intentioned in general from an early age about things, but without any particular focus. I was brought up in a household where it was taken for granted you had a social conscience and cared about other people.

My parents had five children in all but three died: we lived in a small council house and there was hardly any money. We used to get welfare parcels from the Catholics, though how that came about I don't know because we weren't Catholic. I was a big reader: even when I was still at school I'd read anything and everything: tripey romances, adventure stories, Karl Marx and George

Orwell. I enjoyed reading, and I think I got most of my ideas both from family background and from books. I remember my father as an invalid, and when he died I looked after my mother.

Like most girls of my age in this part of the world I left school at fifteen. Then I went to a local college to learn typing, shorthand, commerce studies, and English. My first job was as an office junior for the Coal Board. They kept transferring me from one place to another, and after a while I wanted to give up working for them because transport was so difficult. The job was rather boring too: I felt I wanted to do something better and more interesting, in the sense of having a job more to do with concern for people. One night by chance I was looking in the local evening paper to see what was going: I didn't know what I was looking for, but I saw there was a vacancy for an assistant to a man involved with the miners' Union, and I thought that would be more my line. I worked very happily at that, and as you see I'm still here. My boss died a few years ago: I'd worked for him for a long time, and although we didn't always agree absolutely on everything, I liked him as a man and was in a position where I could feel as though I was at the centre of things politically in the community.

And that's about the extent of my progress. If you look at it one way, it doesn't sound very thrilling or as though it's meant very much. But to me it feels as though I've come on an incredibly long and complex journey inside myself, and arrived at a completely new country, a new way of looking at things. No one could say I was a person of much power or influence, and in my own eyes I'm not. Not the most important person in the world certainly, nor anyone like it. In the Women's Support Groups we don't have leaders or chairpersons: we're all equal. I'm the local Co-ordinator, but that's the only sort of a title that I've got, so you'll have to put me down as that.

Sorry about all the interruptions, but there's so much to attend to. If it's like this now after the strike's over, you can imagine what it was like when it was still on. People still need advice and assistance: they seem to be getting less and less sure every day what steps to take about this that needs doing or that. I think I serve a useful purpose as well as a kind of central information point: if someone wants to know about things that're going on, I usually have a fair idea.

When the strike began I felt at first that to some degree everyone up here had been cocooned against reality. The television had always been accepted as the thing that kept you in touch with the world: people would say 'Let's have the news on to find out what's going on.' It was only as the strike went on that you discovered if you wanted to find out what was going on in your own world, among miners and strikers and in your own life, what you saw on the news wasn't what was going on. It was frightening gradually to realise the extent they selected what they were going to report. Mainly all they were interested in was trouble, and fights between pickets and police. But ideas, pros and cons, the actual arguments that were involved and the rights and wrongs of them, this was something you heard nothing about. What the plan was that the Coal Board had for closing down the pits, how they were throwing men out of work quite deliberately and adding to the unemployment situation in the country, you never heard anything about that. Nor about how the situation had all been carefully planned: the building up of coal stocks, the forming of a mobile police corps, and other forces of 'law and order' – and I'm saying that deliberately, because no one believes it was just made up of the police. The way the strike was engineered to come about, the tricks that were played pretending men were going back to work when they weren't, the idea that pickets were stoning the police without provocation: all such things, if you were here in the centre of it, you couldn't help but realise the country was being fed a completely one-sided picture.

And nothing was said at all about the chicanery they got up to denying Social Security to the families of those who were on strike. The assumption that every striking miner was getting £15 strike pay, and that this could therefore be deducted from the benefit payments – well, I don't know how they could get away with it, and why at the time no one raised any strong protest about it. Miners' wives were supporting their husbands, and they were being penalised for it not only in themselves but through their children too. The Government was actually trying to starve men back to work. That was their policy: kick them and beat them if they demonstrate and protest, and keep up the poverty pressure on them in the hope that if they can't be broken any other way, they'll be broken by their own families. We're supposed to live in a welfare state, but they worked it there was welfare only for some. But I never heard that said on the television news. The miners were put over as a lot of brutal stupid men who were trying to wreck the country. It wasn't that, it was the contrary: the Government of the country was trying to wreck the miners.

The other idea they tried with all the power at their command to sell to people was that it was a political strike, miners were just a lot of sheep blindly following Arthur Scargill. Well I was someone who went round a lot of pits and a lot of villages, and I talked with a lot of miners and I talked with a lot of miners' wives. I went to meetings and I talked, and I went to meetings and I listened and answered questions. And believe me, it wasn't Arthur Scargill's strike. It was those people's strike: theirs, their own. They weren't thoughtless idiots, they were people caring for their futures and the futures of their families, for which they were prepared to go through what they went through for a total of fourteen months. If you can persuade me that hundreds and thousands of people would do that just because Arthur Scargill told them to, I'd think if you believed what you were saying you must be a person who didn't understand anything at all about working people. And I'd say that though the Government may have thought when it was over they'd won, they've misunderstood and misjudged the situation. It's not over and they haven't won: and they've left themselves a residue of bitterness that won't go away for a long long time: I think it'll last for ten years or more, possibly much more.

The police too have got a lot to answer for: they made things worse, a lot worse than they needed to. They were very carefully organised so that wherever you went, say to a pit where for instance they were trying to get scabs in, it wasn't the local police you came up against. You weren't being bullied and pushed around and shouted at by your own local lads. Instead they brought in men from as far away as London so you never knew who they were. Some of them took their numbers off their shoulders and put them in their pockets, several others all had the same numbers on so you'd be confused when it came to trying to report someone. They wouldn't give you their names if you asked them, and if you tried to protest or complain to a senior officer, he'd suddenly run off in a different direction, pretending there was something else urgent he'd got to attend to.

I was on picket lines several times with other women in the Support Groups. We didn't go picketing with the men, we went to places like the factory over at Livermore where they make parts for industrial machinery they use in the pits, where they've got a number of women workers. They were mostly clerical, but they were crossing the picket line to go into the factory, and we decided it was up to us as women to try and talk them out of it. The first time I went, I thought it would be something a bit like a rally and not anything much more than that. But when we got to the gates, so many police suddenly appeared it turned very very frightening. They'd been waiting for us down a side road in their vans. We stood, that's all: a group of women at the gate. The police just charged straight into us, no warning, and knocked several of us flat. I was as much shocked as frightened, I couldn't see why they should be behaving like that. One policeman got my head in an armlock like this, and he dragged me away. It felt as though he was choking me. When I'd recovered I asked an inspector if we could talk to some of the women who were about to go in across the picket line but he refused to allow it. The police formed up round them and marched them straight in.

So the second time we went, at least then I had an idea of what to expect. The atmosphere was even nastier, and as well as the violence the police were extremely abusive and offensive to us. They used foul and filthy language, they shouted things at us that were downright disgusting and inexcusable. Calling us lesbians of course, but making obscene gestures as well and inviting us to come into their vans with them and earn £5. Even nastier were the ones who would talk to you in a friendly fashion, and tell you things like they were really in sympathy with you and the miners, only they had to do their job even though they didn't like it. The ones who were one minute the nicest and friendliest, they were usually the same who when it came to getting the working women in through the picket line, they'd be the ones who lashed out at you and hit you the hardest if you went near them.

What made me feel worst of all though was to see a woman you knew, say who was married to one of your own relatives or friends, whose family you'd helped to feed in the Hall and handed out food parcels and money to – to see her, a particular woman I know, actually cross the picket line and go in to work. That really was the worst feeling. You felt you'd really been taken advantage of, almost as though someone had spat in your face. You'd spent forty-eight weeks of a whole year, your every waking moment devoted to doing what you could to helping people who were standing solid: and then to see someone do that was indescribable, you felt they were degrading you.

– This was the first time in my lifetime that women in general, in this part of the world, became involved in something which was to do with their own lives. A mining community is a very male-orientated society, and I think it was a significant thing that in the strike women became aware of their connections with other women in the community. They had no ready-made structure for them, not like the men and the Union: women had to build their own. It was deliberately informal, but people's response to us from everywhere was wonderful. The money people sent to us came not only from all over this country, but even from places like Germany where their churches sent us money. We bought for example 22,000 turkeys at Christmas so every family we knew of where things were hard at least had a turkey. Christmas altogether was a great lift to everyone's spirits: you felt there was a great solidarity between people. It was hard when the let-down came after that. I don't see there was any alternative to the return to work, but I hope the lessons that were learned, particularly by the women, won't be forgotten. I don't think they will be.

I think the lessons I learned – and I'm not unusual, I was only one of many – were that before it all although I did a lot of reading and thinking, what our society was truly like never made a great impact on me, at least not as far as things outside my own little world were concerned. I'd see Princess Diana on television and all I'd see would be her clothes and her appearance. I'd see the romantic image of a princess, and think it was quite nice and all right, really. It was only as the strike went on that I began to see the reality: I began to see what it was she symbolised and really stood for, which was the privileged section of society, that part of society held up for people's admiration: just something for them to look at, but not because they do any good for others, or take any share in the responsibilities of their sisters.

So it made me look at the women at Greenham Common with totally new eyes too. Up till then I hadn't really given them a thought, or thought it was much to do with us up here. But I learned how to see how all these things are connected with one another. The women at Greenham are women of very strong beliefs, and they're women prepared to sacrifice a lot to make a point about something they believe in. I'm beginning to see the connections between what's happening in the nuclear power industry, what's happening in the coal industry, and what's happening with nuclear weapons. The main one apart from the other obvious ones is people are taking decisions that affect other people's lives and exercise the power of life and death over them, without telling them what they're doing or consulting with them, and being totally secretive and deceitful. I don't know any more than anyone else what happened to that old lady who was murdered, Helen Morrell. But what I have learnt is there's more to it than those in power, including the police, wants to let on: something's being concealed.

I don't like the way our society is governed by people who decide they know what's best for us, and who take that decision themselves and then say to us 'There there, don't worry, we know what's best.' Or that you see women all over the world, in South Africa, if you're black, everywhere all over the world, women treated as though we were inferiors. But to me there's the encouraging thing now that women are beginning to wake up. What they did in the miners' strike was only one example. But if people think now it's over women will go back to sleep and just be docile and obedient again, they'll be making a big mistake.

Part III

The Church Militant
Stephen Kendal

A view from the Board
Brian Dickinson

The Church Militant
Stephen Kendal

I feared the worst. A clergyman who first asked me to meet him 'for a jar' in the bar of his local rugby club. I was wrong.

– I became an industrial chaplain sixteen years ago when I was thirty-five. I spent my first eight years in the steel industry in south Wales, then after that I came here as Industrial Chaplain in the North-Eastern area. I'm employed by the Church, not by the Coal Board. There are times though, if they'll forgive me saying it, when the Board seems to lose sight of that and give the impression I'm dependent on them for my employment. Industrial chaplains are the nearest thing we have to what are called 'worker priests' in some other countries, and it's what I've always wanted to do since I first became ordained. I did have a short period as a parish priest, but I found it unsatisfactory. I don't have a parish or a church, but when necessary fill in occasionally somewhere on a Sunday if for example there's a need for someone because of the local parish priest's illness.

I minister or try to minister to the whole community: and in that sense the whole community is my parish. There are some people I'm sure who'd prefer me to confine myself entirely to welfare work – visiting the sick and injured, trying to save marriages that are on the brink of disruption and that sort of thing, but I don't see the job like that. To me the job is not about proselytising and trying to what they call 'bring the Word' to people: it's more concerned with the practical work of Christianity in the industrial world, trying to work outwards towards Christianity rather than taking religious belief as a starting point.

During the strike things became difficult, but from where I stood and how I saw things, that was inevitable. One of the other industrial chaplains said that in times of fundamental dispute, very few people could afford the luxury of impartiality. The Coal Board seemed to think in some way that I shouldn't take sides, but there could be no question of not doing: I believed that fundamentally one side was in the right and the other in the wrong, and I was prepared to stand up and say so: and I did stand up and say so, whenever the opportunity arose. My only regret is that I wasn't able to achieve anything like as much as I would have wished, or make a wider impact, and I regret that.

Myself and the other industrial chaplains together issued a press statement, calling for negotiation. Several of the local management Coal Board members weren't at all happy about it, nor were they about both the implicit and the explicit criticism of them. Some of them thought I was far exceeding my remit, and said so in no uncertain terms: we had some quite warm exchanges. They were entitled to their opinion, but I would have thought more of them if they'd also spoken out about other things too which I knew they were not happy about. For instance, the bussing-in of miners into pits, to try and give the impression there was a will to return to work by large numbers of them, was not something which was at all popular with quite a few members of the Board. They thought it was provocative, and in some cases deceitful, and they were not happy about it. I felt and said that if they felt like that they should say so, and help to make an impression on those higher up than they were. Because of my position, during the strike I wasn't able to say things as constantly publicly critical of senior management as I would have wished, but I did make my views very clear to them regularly in private.

If you'd come here to my house to see me three years ago, you'd have met someone who believed there was a good future for the coal industry. Then I was quite excited about it, I believed both that there was a concensus between management and men, and that that was the right way to run the industry. I was living in cloud-cuckoo-land, I didn't at that time know about the Ridley plan, and I didn't know what was coming. I believed that our society, even if it had a Conservative government at its head, was at heart a caring one, and that what divisions there were were largely to do with method rather than with principle. The Ridley plan was a Conservative Policy Group report, drawn up when they were in opposition, about proposals for denationalising industries, particularly the coal industry, and breaking the power of the Unions.

When Ian MacGregor was appointed Chairman of the National Coal Board, I was aware of what he'd done when he was at the British Steel Corporation, and I was under the impression he'd start his cuts at senior management level, and try to get that side of things more up to date. I thought he'd been appointed because, according to the Conservatives' lights, he was a good experienced business-man. I completely failed to see how much he was going to be operating hand in glove with the Government. His main job was to break the influence and power of the National Union of Miners. I truly didn't see that, or the even wider determination of the Tories to smash trades unionism itself. Revision and rearrangement: I thought those things would be among MacGregor's aims: but intent on destruction, for a political purpose, that I didn't see. So when it became clear what the Government was up to, how determined it was on confrontation on its own chosen battleground, and on fighting to a finish to achieve what it wanted, I don't see how anyone could not have been on one side or the other about it. But as I say if you'd come to see me three years ago, I think you'd have found someone politically naïve, someone who didn't know people in government could be quite as evil as they were.

Yes I admit it, evil is a very strong word to use, perhaps specially so when it's used by a clergyman who's not being lighthearted about it. But I do believe there was evil, blatant evil, in what went on. Government saying the quarrel was purely between the Coal Board and the miners, and it wasn't going to interfere in any way. That was untrue, and those who were saying it knew it: they were the very people who were day by day interfering and controlling what was going on. I also think using the police as a political tool, using them as a weapon of fear and violence, was evil too. I don't think anyone could or should refrain from speaking up and condemning it. They were a state police force: put into riot gear, making cavalry charges, using their batons, and beating people. That that sort of thing happened on the streets and in the villages of this country was shocking and horrifying. People were arrested and criminalised, and the courts were used to prevent their freedom of movement by the application of bail conditions which were quite exceptional. Not one but hundreds of decent working men were found guilty of offences that in many cases they didn't understand or even know existed. A typical one was the offence of besetting, which was first used against people in the summer of the year of the strike. It was done quite cynically: it was something somebody discovered as a section of an act of 1875 I believe it was. The actual offence is called 'watching and besetting': when I first heard it I couldn't find it mentioned in a single law book or reference book in the public library. I even went and searched through dictionaries and handbooks for lawyers themselves. By the end, over 200 men were charged with it.

I could barely understand what was being allowed to happen, and without people rising up in protest about it. We've been told for years about how proud we should be of our press freedom and how it defends the rights of individuals. But nothing I read anywhere said anything about this, nobody influential and no newspaper had the courage to denounce what was happening. It was almost as if we were at war, and any point of reasonable argument was treason. The previous time it happened was in the war against the Argentines over the Falklands: all the newspapers ganged together then to sing a song of jingoism, completely swamping any discussion or argument about whether what we were doing was right or justified. Anyone who protested, even in the slightest way, was attacked for doing so. And then in the strike the same thing was done to a section of our own countrymen. We were told the miners were attacking and trying to wreck the state: and it was the exact opposite that was true. The Government was attacking the miners and wanted to wreck them, to break them so their Union wouldn't ever be in a position again to oppose the Government.

When we talked about the violence on the picket lines, and there was violence on both sides, I'm trying not to apportion degrees of blame for it. I think for a start it's got to be remembered miners have always been somewhat violent because of the very nature of their job. I don't think that the way the strike was policed took this properly into account: or if it did, it was done in such a way as to suggest there was almost a relishing by the police of the fighting that did occur. There's no doubt that a great deal of police behaviour was deliberately provocative. It's only now, long afterwards, that we're hearing stories about them bursting into people's houses, on the grounds they were looking for men who'd committed offences on the picket line. We're now hearing stories about them chasing men down the streets in their own towns and villages, purely and simply to attack them, not merely to catch them with as little force as possible. There was a low violence threshold everywhere: you couldn't expect men as bitter and angry and frustrated as the miners were not to react when they saw a threatening demonstration in front of them by police, which signalled what certainly appeared to be the start of aggression. There were many instances where men were behaving in a quite peaceful fashion until the police arrived. My feeling is that a great deal of the violence could have been avoided if that's what the police had genuinely wanted to happen.

– I think the end of the strike was a profoundly sad occasion. A once very great and very proud union was

utterly humiliated. No genuine solution had ever been
sought by the Government at all, they wanted to give the
NUM a mauling and they succeeded. But I think it's the
duty of Government, in a country such as ours where
we profess to believe in democracy, to find compromises
between different points of view. It's surely the job of
Government to try to get each section of the community
to live in harmony with the others. But I don't believe it
was ever the intention of Government to do that in this
case at any time, and what's happened since confirms it.
There are strong rumours, more than rumours, that they're
helping the breakaway Union of Democratic Miners to set
themselves up, and to keep the miners divided between
that and the NUM.

In the future, attempts are going to be made I'm sure
to portray the strike as an example of the Union Leader,
Arthur Scargill, leading his blind followers by the nose for
his own personal aggrandisement. Anyone who comes to
this part of the world won't find much support for that
view, I think. They'll more likely be very surprised at
the respect and affection which the man commands.
Most people agree he made mistakes and that he let himself be outmanoeuvred by the Government. But he
still commands a great deal of respect: I think it's quite
remarkable how people are not bitter towards him in any
way.

Another thing I think is that the whole population has
to accept responsibility for running the country not just as
this Government is doing for the benefit of the few, but
for the good of everybody. On the whole people aren't
looking at the country's problems, they're trying to pretend
they don't exist. Building leisure centres and all the rest
of it is fiddling while Rome burns, and meantime our
economic situation is getting worse and worse: we're not
competing in world markets at all. We haven't any real
future to offer people unless the Government gives a lead
in trying to re-establish a kind of society that people
want to co-operate with and live in. When the churches

produced as they did a little while ago their report on the inner cities, it just wasn't good enough that politicians in Government dismissed them as a few meddling Marxists talking about things they didn't understand. In fact the churches should have been much more critical about Government than they were. They should have been the Church Militant. They should have pointed out the Government had a duty, as well as an economic necessity, to provide employment for people: and that they were failing in their duty when they didn't even attempt to do it.

When I was ordained as a young man, I never dreamed the day would come again when I'd see food kitchens for miners. At the welfare halls around all the villages here, to see the Women's Support Groups every day making meals and giving out food parcels: I never believed I'd see it. The old naked Victorian charity idea in action, it was appalling that we'd been driven to that. If the Government doesn't take responsibility for women and children who were suffering hardship and deprivation, like the miners' families were, through no fault whatsoever of their own, if the Government doesn't even accept it has a responsibility to be concerned, what on earth are we coming to?

It was all bad and it was all wrong, but above all it was all desperately sad. There was nothing romantic about the strike to those who lived up here in this part of the world and went through it. There was real continuous suffering, and there was deliberate cruelty perpetrated against those who had to live on Social Security. It was deliberately cruel to try to force a man back to work by making his wife and children go short of food.

The net result was, and it'll continue to be in the minds of a lot of people, particularly young people, a feeling that authority is a bad and uncaring thing, which should wherever possible be avoided. This is a sign of a sick society, but I don't see any indication anywhere of anybody in Government even wanting to do anything about it. The police in particular have a lot of ground to make up. They lost a lot of good will. Our society's based, or we've always been told it was based on, policing by consent, not on policing by force or fear. In the strike we weren't far from a police state, and it seems certain we can't ever go back to the kind of situation we had before. People won't forget the sight of police convoys in their villages, strange policemen milling round their streets in their hundreds, and villages in turn being cut off and isolated by police forces.

It'll be a long time too for the press and the media to recover respect and credibility. Only one newspaper consistently reported the strike fairly, and that was the *Financial Times*. But you can't blame the miners for saying *all* the press was against them: how many miners read the *Financial Times*? The *Nine O'Clock News* and the *News at Ten*, both of them did themselves no good at all with their heavily slanted approach. Person after person I've talked to, at all levels in the community, now says quite regularly and as an accepted thing 'You can't believe anything that's on the television.' Both television news programmes had an inbuilt bias because the news was put together in selection and editing in the south of the country, by southerners, and with the southern audience in view. What was happening in the strike was something that was going on in a foreign country, 'up there in the north'. These weren't 'our' people, these weren't a selection of the population who had anything to do with 'us'. The attitude was: 'Those people up there, why are they creating so much bother?'

I hope the desperate sadness and bitterness which still remains won't be forgotten or overlooked. It's not enough to do as the Government did, looking on it as teaching part of the population a lesson. There's a lesson for the Government too, and it's both a practical one and a moral one. Not 'No man is an island', but that all of us live on the same island. We're all dependent upon one another, we all need one another, we all have a responsibility towards one another. A government that tries to teach flat contradiction of that is one of poor quality and dreadful poverty of spirit. And it'll lead its whole population into poverty.

A view from the Board
Brian Dickinson

– Yes, it'd be correct to describe me as a member of the NCB Area Management Board. I've been in the coal industry all my life, and I started at fourteen when I left school. My whole family background is mining, I lived in a colliery village, my father worked in the local pit and so did most of my male relatives. I started in the time office, handing out the clocking-on cards: I was the office boiler-stoker, tea-maker, first-aid attendant and everything else that needed doing. Then I moved on into the accounts department where I was involved with wages. All my work was nearly always in the office, on the clerical side, but I went underground fairly frequently to estimate perform-ance levels and things of that kind. I've never seriously considered leaving the industry or going into something else: now I've only two years to go before my retirement, or I could finish a little before that, perhaps next year. Perhaps it'd be best to describe my job as on the industrial relations side, put it like that. It's chiefly concerned with personnel management, allocation of housing, workers' transport, training and so on: and it's also involved a lot of dealing with disputes and negotiating with the unions. I've enjoyed it very much, all my life: but recently it's been rather different in nature. Inevitably it's been affected by the disastrous events of the strike, and by the devastating results which that's had on relations with the workforce. It's all left a dreadful legacy, and the job is now far more difficult and complicated.

I was in right from before the time of nationalisation, and I saw the unity which grew up and developed after that between men and management and the unions. Anybody couldn't help but feel sad that that's lost, and it isn't like that any more. There were some great trades union leaders in those days among the miners: Sam Watson was one, he was always speaking and writing about the need to maintain good relationships in the industry. He was an influential man in the Labour party and his ideal was to create a truly socialist society: he felt that could only be done if aspirations were tempered with an awareness of the needs of all. I remember he wrote about the 'economic boundaries' of the coal industry, and for the need to keep it within those limits. Some people would say that over the years it became almost cosy, that the boundaries have been exceeded: and that being economic as well as productive has tended to become ignored. In recent years, in trying to cut back to realistic limits, I'd agree that perhaps what has been done has been done too fast and has gone too far. Some would say so. Certainly it hasn't been done, much of it, with the identity of interest for everyone in the industry, which was always the guiding principle before. The industry of course has always been subsidised: and much of the hardship that happened when pits were closed, as they inevitably had to be when they were no longer producing coal, was absorbed and cushioned by the rest of the industry.

I do still believe there are sufficient jobs in the future in the industry for those who want to stay on in it. But promotion prospects have slowed down: the situation at present is that recruiting is at a standstill. But I hope that's no more than a hiccup. Perhaps it'll be a long one, yes: and to be realistic I'd have to say recovery might take as long as a generation. But I hope not. I'd like to say there'd definitely be a future in it for a young entrant, say a school leaver: our tentative future planning does have built into it the need for new recruitment. But in this part of the world unfortunately we can't at this time offer employment. I'm one of those though who's hopeful that the future will improve.

The whole image of the industry is now very much tarnished, I agree: so the sooner we can get the recent troubles behind us and work together for the future the better. There used to be a great *esprit de corps* at every level in the coal mining: miners were special people, everyone knew it and respected them. A lot of that has been very badly damaged, because things were not handled in the way they should have been. This has caused a lot of bitterness, and to some of us it's a source of great sadness.

Miners are and always have been first-class people, with good and responsible work attitudes. They do a hard job and they do it conscientiously and with a fine spirit. But in some ways their attitudes have worked to their own detriment. Their loyalty to their Union, and their willingness to suffer on behalf of their communities, as was shown in the strike, was, and I think no one would argue about it, admirable: but it did do them harm. The suggestion that the Coal Board deliberately tried to break the Union is one that it's understandable some people should make. But it became essential, or at least this was the view from the Board, that so much damage was being caused to the industry that it was essential to get the men back to work. I wasn't by any means alone in wanting someone to take hold of the dispute by the scruff of the neck, and see what could be done. I can't be more specific about who I mean by 'someone', but it must be obvious. But no one interceded, the dispute was allowed to drag on and on and on without any attempt being made reaching a compromise solution: and that was dreadfully harmful not only to the industry and to its history of industrial relations which it had every reason to be proud of, but also to the mining communities with the indignities which were heaped upon them.

I agree too that certain things were done which would appear as being deliberately provocative: yes, bussing men to the pit was one. In my purely personal opinion, that sort of thing was right out of character with the Coal Board's management style in the past. But we did what we had to do, and whether we were right or wrong will be for other people later to decide. It was a common criticism at the time to say we did exactly as we were told to: the feeling was that we had to get the strike ended, and then go on from there into a situation where reasonable discussions could take place. That the National Union of Mineworkers could ever come to look upon the Coal Board as an enemy is something I could simply never have imagined when nationalisation began. It's disastrous, and that's the only word, disastrous, that the situation which now obtains has occurred: I'm very saddened indeed at the end of my working life to be leaving at such a stage in the industry's history.

Why it happened and why we've come to this state is undoubtedly because of the rate of the run-down. We've been closing pits for a long time, all my lifetime: in this industry you reach a point with certain pits when there's no more coal in them, you have to shut them. But what's not been sufficiently emphasised is the prospecting side, the looking for new coal. Equally I think not sufficient attention's been paid to the social consequences of the loss of jobs. It used to be there were always other jobs to go to, but in these times and in this area, you look around and you see there's a gradual and now very serious decline in future employment prospects for anyone. This area has one of the highest unemployment proportions of anywhere in the country.

It's understandable the Union reached a point when they felt the closure programme had gone not only too fast but too far, and that if they didn't make a stand when a certain pit was closed, in what some people will have seen as a very provocative manner – that if they didn't take a stand, they'd never have any future credibility. There were all sorts of additional political overtones and undertones to it, including for instance the programme of considerable expansion in the number of nuclear power stations: and none of that sort of thing was going to encourage the miners to believe that anyone was paying much concern for their future.

Of course as a Coal Board official it's impossible for me to be objective, I see things from our side just as the Union people see things from theirs, and everything that has so far been written has inevitably been biased towards one side or the other. But the main failure it seems to me was one of communication, and I would say that much of that failure was undoubtedly by the Board. It failed to communicate to both the miners and to the public that they were sufficiently committed to the future welfare of the mining community, and they certainly failed to express sufficient concern about it.

The coal industry is, and it always has been, an industry of very high feelings and great emotion. None of this is necessarily all bad: there's a great solidarity comes from sharing hard and dangerous work with your mates. And the industry's always been one that was politically alive and aware. But I don't remember a time before when it was as sadly polarised as it is now, and this came about because of this failure of communication I've spoken of. At all costs somehow we should have kept on talking. More effort might have been made in one direction if there could have been communication directly to the miners themselves. But the tradition has always been that the unions was the main channel of communication: the unions in fact in some senses was almost part of management. They carried out that role certainly in the personnel area for us, and we had wonderful relations. By-passing the leaders did look like trying to undermine their traditional role, and it caused great hostility. Letters written direct to individual members of the workforce for instance: I can't really feel that anyone could have believed that sort of action could improve things in any way. There were 'mail shots' from the Chairman to every employee: and to any-one who knows miners, it's difficult to see them responding to that sort of thing. How can they be expected to identify with an extremely highly paid businessman from abroad, rather than with their own Union? I'm not sure that kind of approach could ever work. But if it was decided to try it, in my personal view letters might have stood more chance of having an effect if they'd come from the men's own immediate bosses, whom most of them had known personally for most of their working lives.

The manager of a colliery regularly goes underground, he knows the operational problems, he knows the geography of the place, and there's been friendship and trust built up between him and the men who work under him over the years. The relationship is soundly based on joint understanding of working difficulties and problems. The men look on their manager as one of them, and in most cases they have a mutual knowledge of one another's backgrounds not just as workers but as people. This was an asset the Coal Board didn't take advantage of from early in the strike, and this came from higher-up management level. Whether it was because they were ignorant of the relationship, or whether it was because they thought it wasn't worth paying attention to, I don't know. But it was there and it could have been used, and a lot of people feel it should have been used.

Another example would be in how violence is now being dealt with. Mining has always been a very tough physical job, and one of the things that it's always spawned is a certain amount of physical aggression. But in the past, in the majority of cases this has always been dealt with within the colliery itself, between men who know one another. I'm not entirely happy with the present policy on dismissals at all, and there are some other people in the Board who also feel it hasn't been handled right. Obviously I can't make a statement on behalf of the Board itself, but I would be prepared to say some of us feel we might have done better if we'd been allowed to handle local difficulties. We could have done it in a less remote way and one that might have been more acceptable. I am inclined to believe there could have been a rather more forgiving attitude, yes.

Other things that have not been entirely satisfactory in the way they were handled were to do with pit closures, and their extent and rate. I do feel it's been very unfortunate that statements were issued about intentions which were then later revised. Certain pits were told straight out they were facing closure: others were not exactly guaranteed they were secure, but certainly were allowed to continue under the impression they were. There were then instances of sudden announcements about imminent closure, and they were totally unexpected, no inkling of them had been given. It can't then be entirely unexpected that that sort of thing leads not only to a furore in the immediate area of the pit, but to a great fanning of flames of suspicion about other assurances the Coal Board has given. Things really should be handled better than that. You have to admit if you work for it that the Coal Board has lost some of its credibility not only with its workers, but also additionally with some of its potential customers. It's not very easy to persuade people in industry to invest in large-scale schemes for coal burning equipment when the industry's in this kind of state. And I'd add that the emerging of a new union for miners hasn't helped the situation. An impression is abroad that the NUM's not only been beaten over the strike but it's now having its nose rubbed in the dirt by the management being prepared to negotiate with the new Union. It's a very prickly and difficult situation.

– The official policy of the Coal Board about dismissals and reinstatements is this. In virtually all cases which were what you might call trivial offences, minor thefts and so on, most of those dismissed for this reason have been re-employed. Only one or two were very serious in our view: but where people took large quantities of coal for commercial disposal, we didn't offer them their jobs back.

As far as the violence cases were concerned, we have not reinstated any of them. Some of them were very extreme indeed: in some cases men were found guilty of inflicting grievous bodily harm, and we felt we had to draw the line where violence was involved. This is nothing new, it's always been standard practice in the past. If someone committed an act of violence and was sent to prison for it, afterwards he got the sack. Yes it's true that we have sacked people in cases of violence during the strike, who were subsequently acquitted by the courts. But we dealt with these on the evidence available to us, some of which was not available to the court, and we operated our own rules. There are bound to be what look like inequalities and unfairnesses, but the Coal Board takes the line that it is after all the employer: and any employer is entitled to get rid of someone who behaves in a way which is beyond the bounds of acceptable behaviour.

I don't see how we could be expected to declare general amnesty for everybody irrespective of what they'd done. We have to reserve the right to take certain decisions which we feel are correct. I personally think it would be more sensible to have a review of each individual case, one by one on its merits, say perhaps by a committee composed of officials from all sides including the Union. But this is only a personal view: it's a very difficult area indeed, and I could well see that suggestion creating more problems than it solved.

I agree there's room for improvement on all sides: I agree that certainly there are some aspects of what you might call the residue of the strike, in the attitude of the Coal Board, that are quite some way from being satisfactory. I still wish there could be more talking between management and Union, and I don't mean shouting or name-calling, though there'd now inevitably be plenty of that. But I'm not alone in the Board in regretting every single instance which now occurs which seems willy-nilly to widen the rift between the Board and the Union: as I said to you earlier, it's not something I've ever before been used to in all my working life.

Part IV

The way it looks from here

Paul Dennis, school-leaver
Philip James, policeman
Mary Edwards, schoolteacher
Eddie Vernon, shopkeeper
Jimmy Barrett, journalist
Elaine Houghton, school-leaver

Envoi

Paul Dennis, school-leaver

– I'm 16, I left school in the summer, I haven't had a job since then. I've got one CSE in geography. My dad's a miner, he was one of those who came out on strike with the rest at the pit: he stayed out till the very last day, he didn't scab, nothing like that, he's not that sort of person. I don't know why anyone would scab, I think there was only one boy at our school whose father did that: the rest of us, we were all solid.

I think yes I would have gone down the mine if there'd been jobs. My dad always said I ought to try something else, but I'd never really thought about it because I think it was a good job. They're not taking anyone of my age on at the moment though, and anyhow if I couldn't go to Red Hill I'd not like to go anywhere else. I sign on each week to say that I'm available for work, but so far I've not had nothing offered me except a job right over the other side of Peterlee. They sent me to see a man who said he was starting up a business, I think it was to do with soft drinks in cans, he wanted someone as a packer. When I went in to see him all he said was the employment people had made a mistake, he'd told them he wanted a girl school-leaver, not a boy. My feeling is he was offering light work, perhaps part-time or something of that sort: he'd be able to pay less if it was a girl.

I've seven friends from my class all in the same boat, I think between the seven of us three have been for jobs but nothing's so far come up for any of us. I'm getting a bit fed up with it, we all are. One of my friends thought he'd have a try for the army, he wasn't keen on it but he said he couldn't think what else to do. He went along to the recruiting office and they gave him some tests and said they'd let him know. That was three months ago, I shouldn't think he'll hear anything now.

Being out of work hasn't been too bad so far, but it gets a bit boring: you feel sometimes you'd like to be being in work, even if it was only sweeping roads or something of that sort. I think what the Government ought to do is work out something that'd give us proper work so we could feel we were being useful and also earn our living. At the present it's like you're waiting for someone to do you a favour.

I don't go a lot on those things they call training schemes, they only last a year. A friend of mine went on one, it was in a meat pie factory. He spent the whole day carting carcasses from vans into the cold store. He said he couldn't see what it was he was being trained to do. The bloke he was working for said he ought to be grateful to have any kind of a job. He said there was no future in it as far as he could see, I think I would have felt the same.

In the evenings you go to the sports club and muck about. That's all right for the ones who like playing games, but I never did, I was never any good at them. A thing I don't like is that the library closes at seven o'clock, that's one of the few places I really like to go. I like it because I like looking at books, and also because in our house my sister has the television on all the time. She watches *Emmerdale Farm* and that *Brookside* and all those stupid serials, and there's nowhere else to sit except in the kitchen or upstairs in the bedroom.

A thing I don't like at all is the police. There's a friend of mine he's got an old banger of a motor car: and sometimes four or five of us go out in an evening in it, say perhaps go over to one of the other villages to see our friends. We don't go often, only about once a week, because we can only afford to do it when we've got enough between us to give him something towards the petrol. If you go up over Borough Bridge way, that's a favourite spot for the police to wait. Nine times out of ten if they see a load of young lads in a motor car they stop you: they ask you what you're doing, where you're going and that, who the car belongs to, where you got the money from for the petrol and all the rest of it. We were coming back one night, it must have been around pub closing time, they stopped us and made three of us breathe in a breathalyser. There was nothing wrong because we hadn't been drinking. They didn't say sorry or nothing of that sort, they just said 'Get off home quick and don't let's catch you again.' The way they said it, they make you feel you've done something. You daren't say anything back to them: they look at you very hard, you think the more you were to say the more trouble they'd try and get you in.

The way it looks from here, most of all I'd say living in Red Hill is boring because there's nothing for young people. I heard somebody say on television one night that people ought to go to different parts of the country and look for jobs. Next day I asked the employment people where they suggested I should go, and if they'd give me money to go and look for work. They said it was up to me: I should do it first and if I could prove to them I'd made a serious effort, they might give me some money afterwards or tell me how to get it back from the Social.

I don't know what's going to happen. Most of all I'd have liked to have stayed at school, but I wasn't bright enough.

Philip James, *policeman*

– The most important thing most people didn't understand was the feeling the police had amongst themselves towards each other. We kept hearing all the time in the strike and afterwards about the miners' loyalty to the Union, but

you didn't hear anything at all on the police side about
policemen's loyalty to one another. Just as much as the
miners did they felt they were sticking together with their
mates: that spirit of helping your mates is something which
is very strong in the police force. I don't care where you
go anywhere in the country, you'll find the same thing,
that one policeman will stand by another policeman.
If there are twenty policemen in a tight spot somewhere about something and another twenty policemen
can see them, they'll go to their aid. They don't start asking questions 'Hello, hello, what's all this here about
then?' All they see is twenty other policemen being
roughed up, and they go straight in and help them.
They leave the questioning about what it's about until
later.

There were times in the strike when it got very very
nasty indeed. There were clear laws for what pickets could
do and what they couldn't do, and how many of them
there should be. There was deliberate flouting of those
laws by flying pickets as they were called, and mobs of
miners. Sometimes it wasn't funny at all. You might be
standing there and there was say a hundred of you at the
start, and you thought you'd got more than enough of
you to cope with it if there was any trouble. And then
more and more people would start to arrive, and they'd
keep on coming until you started to realise you were out-
numbered five or even ten to one. Then someone would
throw things: bricks and stones and sometimes things I
don't like to mention were thrown at you. It might be
only slight at first, but then others would begin doing
the same thing because you weren't giving them any
retaliation.

I never saw it anywhere at any time, where it was the
police that started the trouble. I think people don't know
sufficiently what a lot the police put up with first before
they even moved in the direction of the people causing the
trouble. We stood with our shields and we took a great
deal of abuse and shouting at us: it was only when it was

starting to get out of hand that we were given the order to calm things down. Policemen don't go round looking for fights, it wouldn't make sense for them to do that because there are much much fewer of us than there are of the general population. If we didn't have the majority of the population on our side, we'd soon be in bad trouble. You take a place like the village: if they suddenly decided one day they weren't going to have police here any more, they could declare the village a no-go area, like the sort of thing that happens in Northern Ireland. Thousands of police would have to be brought in to restore order: and they'd have to be brought in from somewhere else. So as they were moved away from wherever it was, then the people there could start creating in their turn. So it has to be the general population's consent.

It's true strangers were brought in to particular trouble spots, police strangers I mean. This was partly because you couldn't have one policeman in two places at once and when reinforcements were needed you had to have them available quickly. There was also the feeling, though we weren't ever officially told it in so many words, that after the strike we would have to police our own communities again, and it wouldn't make for easy relationships if we'd been on actual fighting terms with our own people that we had to move about among every day. That seems to me to have been a sensible policy.

It wasn't always appreciated there were some of the men on strike who it wouldn't have made no difference to them, whatever the police did those men were there looking for trouble. There were certain men known to us as professional agitators: you'd see them one day outside the gates at Waddell Moor, then the next day you'd be on duty somewhere miles away and they were there. We used to have a joke about some of them: we'd look at a situation where it looked there was going to be trouble, and we'd have a guess at how many men were there. Then someone would say 'I reckon John Jones will be coming in for this one', John Jones being the name of one of the really bad lads who thought he was somebody special. Somebody else would say 'Oh no, I don't think this one is up to John Jones level, he'll be over at so-and-so, they've got a much bigger demonstration on there today.' Then a sergeant would come down and he'd say 'There's trouble over at such-and-such, it sounds like it'll be a John Jones.' We used to have bets on which people would turn up to the place where we were. I can tell it to you now and smile about it, but at the time it was serious: if you saw John Jones arrive you knew you were going to be in for a scrap.

But I think most people have forgotten the troubles now, they just want to get on with their lives and I don't think there's much bad feeling left. You could say in certain cases and certain instances perhaps some policemen were a little bit excessive in how they behaved: but if they were it was always because they'd been given a hard time themselves. Policemen are only human beings, they can only put up with so much. They do the best they can under very difficult circumstances and I think the general public by and large appreciates that. I haven't noticed at our station, and I bet you wouldn't find one anywhere in the country where they had, that there's been any falling off in the number of calls for assistance the public make to the police. They still know the police can be relied on to come to the assistance of anyone who's been injured or robbed, or is in trouble in any way. We're not in anything like as bad a state of relationships as some people try to make out.

I don't have any regrets about the strike, except I think people got away with a lot of things they shouldn't have been allowed to get away with. When you knew one of your friends that'd been knocked down and set on and kicked, and then you saw the men who'd done it walking free from court because they'd got a clever barrister who'd been able to persuade the court there wasn't sufficient evidence for a conviction, it made you feel very sour. And then the prosecution felt if they couldn't get a conviction in one case, it wasn't worth their while pursuing say perhaps another fifty others. I think that was wrong, I think those who committed offences should have been punished for them, but there was far too much in the other direction. But if it all adds up in the end to restoring relations with the community, I suppose you could say in the long run it's probably better it should be that way. But there's still a good deal of feeling among policemen on that subject, they feel in a way they've been let down. They took the brunt of all the unpopularity, not only from the striking miners but afterwards from a lot of other people, and some of us we do, we feel very sour about it.

Mary Edwards, schoolteacher

– I teach at a junior school, where the ages go up to eleven of mixed boys and girls. I've been here five years, but I don't come from this area, I'm from the Midlands myself.

A number of things surprise me after the strike. The chief one is how deep people's feelings still run. There was a lot of bitterness after the strike because the miners didn't really achieve anything: quite a number of parents felt that after all they'd suffered they should have gone on until they'd won. They said if only solidarity had been more complete, they would have achieved their objective. Personally I don't think they would, I think the Government was too set on its course. I think it felt the day had to come when there was a confrontation. I don't know much about the ins and outs, but it's definitely struck me since that they'd prepared for it, and they took the Union by surprise. It's not really for me to say, I'm not from a mining family: but I did get the impression the Union had been over-confident in some respects. They'd succeeded in their strikes in 1972 and 1974, and even this Government had backed down rather than face a strike with them a few years ago. So in a way the Union got a false idea of its own strength, and in the end I think that was the reason for them getting beaten. They hadn't taken into account how determined the Government was going to be this time, nor how carefully it'd made preparations.

As far as the children at school were concerned, in my class half of them at least came from families where either their fathers worked down the mine, or uncles or other close relatives did, and so they felt very keenly what was going on. And I felt very sorry indeed for some of them whose fathers were among those who went on working. Children can be very cruel to one another: we had rather a lot of trouble in the middle of the strike. The situation nationally was getting ugly, the children were seeing scenes on the television news that aroused very strong passions. The worst thing that could happen to any child would be when some of the others ganged up in the playground and shouted at them and bullied them. The word they were using of course was 'scab'. At first they used to chant 'Your dad's a scab, your dad's a scab' and they stamped their feet in a rhythm with it like that. It was really frightening at times to hear it.

Quite often a child didn't know why the others were shouting at it, and what the implications were of what they were shouting. One little girl, her father was on strike but he went into the pit, with the full knowledge and approval of the Union, to provide what was called 'safety cover'. That's basic maintenance work to ensure the safety of the pit while it's idle. But some child or other got hold of this knowledge, and brought it into the school, and accused the child that her father was scabbing, when he was doing nothing of the kind. The child didn't know enough about it to be able to put up any defence, and more than once that girl was reduced to tears because of the baiting by her school mates.

We had a lot of discussion in the staff room about how

we could best help those children whose fathers were scabbing. I think the families of the striking miners quite often put their children up to what they were doing: I've no proof of this, but I know that in close circles like miners' villages, everybody knows everybody else's business. The staff tried not to take sides, but of course everyone did, and the majority were definitely on the side of the miners.

We also had one or two unfortunate incidents with the police. They could have been a lot less heavy-handed than they were. There was one morning when the television news the night before had shown a very large-scale fight in Nottinghamshire between police and strikers' pickets, and another place where stones and bricks were thrown at a bus taking men into a pit when they wanted to go back to work. This was more or less the sole topic of conversation in the school that day morning: and at dinner time there just happened to be two policemen outside the school standing by their patrol car. Some of the kids were jeering at them, shouting and calling them 'pigs'. Quite the simplest thing would have been if the two policemen had got in their car and driven away, giving the impression they hadn't heard. But they didn't do that, they started walking round among the children and ticking them off. You really can't talk sensibly with children of that age when they're in an excited mood, so of course before long there were more and more children gathering round and shouting at the policemen. They then made it worse by radioing for back-up, and another patrol car arrived. One of the senior staff at the school phoned up the police station and told them what was occurring, and suggested the police should be told to withdraw. In a short time they must have received that message because they went away. But later in the afternoon a police chief inspector came up to the school, and there was a big row. He blamed the staff for egging the children on: he demanded to have the whole school, teachers and pupils, called together so he could give them a piece of his mind. Fortunately he wasn't given permission to do so, and in a few days' time tempers had cooled down. Obviously the police were very sensitive about their image.

If you live and work in a community like this, you're bound to be affected by the sad things you see and hear. A very large number of people had a very hard time in the strike, it ought to be made plain that they're still having a very hard time indeed trying to catch up financially.

Eddie Vernon, shopkeeper

– I've lived here all my life, this shop was my father's before me. It used to be an ordinary tobacco shop, but a few years back I branched out into newspapers and periodicals. It's always been my policy to try and plough money back into the firm: it gives a living to the wife and me, but we're both getting on a bit now. If somebody gave me a decent offer for it today, I'd sit down and consider it very seriously.

In a place like this this sort of shop is at the heart of things, and we've always felt ourselves to be a little centre of the community. Every day people come in and tell us bits of news: some of it's not much more than gossip, and you have to say a bit of it is downright mischievous. But on the whole this is a news centre for the village. We know who's ill, who's on holiday, where they are and when they're coming back and all that sort of thing. We also get to hear a fair bit which we don't pass on.

We used to enjoy it much more than we do now. But I think everyone looks back to the good old days and they always look a bit rosier than they actually were don't they? But we've said it to each other a lot lately, we seem to be hearing mostly very sad stories and not many cheerful ones. There's an atmosphere somehow in the village that it's hard to describe. When I was young there were hard

times too in those days: when I first started working for
my father here at this counter, we used to have a notebook
we wrote down things in that people had had, and they
would pay us off a bit at a time. If someone was in
difficulties, we'd give them credit because they were people
we knew and who lived all around. But now things don't
seem to have quite the same amount of personal feel to
them. I don't think most are as happy and easy-going about
things as they used to be. People are worried about things,
you can see it in their faces when they come in through
that door. It might be a man's wife or it might be the
man himself, but you get almost so you can tell in ad-
vance, as soon as you look at them, they've been made
redundant or they've been told they must choose between
redundancy and transfer to another pit out of the area.
Employment and how long it'll last for everyone, that's the
big question. Everyone seems they're carrying a big
weight on their shoulders: and they are of course, they
are.

In the strike it was almost sometimes quite jolly, it
reminded me of the war: there was the feeling that everyone was in it together, and that in the end we'd come
through it and win. We'd have women in here who we'd
known for years, they'd never had much to say for themselves and then suddenly one day they'd come in and
they'd be buzzing with excitement about what they were
doing with the Support Group: how they were collecting
money, how they were on shifts at the Welfare Hall giving
out dinners for hundreds of people. You were amazed:
these were women you'd always thought never had much
in their lives at all, and then they were suddenly sparking
with enthusiasm and laughing and joking.

There was a terrific feeling of let-down when the strike
ended and everyone went back to work. We had more
than a few people in here standing crying. When the
rumour started to go around that Red Hill might be closed,
everyone was very very shocked. They wanted to think of
something they could do to stop it, but they were com-

pletely powerless to do anything but what they're still doing, which was wait and see and they knew it. It isn't very nice to see.

As far as this business here in this shop goes, I think it will make a big difference to us if they do shut Red Hill down. If people transfer I think it will take all the stuffing out of the community. Or if they take redundancy, I think before long they'll start to drift away. It won't be because they want to, a lot of them have never lived anywhere else: but they'll have to think about their children and what's going to happen to them in the future. There certainly aren't no employment prospects here. It's a very bad outlook. I can remember ten years ago or so when this was a boom area, so the Coal Board was telling everyone: the future was assured in our lifetime. But everyone doubts that now. No one knows what's going to happen, and I think there's a feeling that people in the rest of the country don't care. I'd say the main feeling people have here is they've been abandoned, and no one's going to put themselves out on their behalf. People feel they're powerless little cogs in a big machine.

Jimmy Barrett, journalist

– I'm not now, but at the time of the strike I was a reporter on one of the local papers in the area: one of those people I was always told who wasn't giving a fair picture of things, writing downright lies, only putting things unfavourable to the miners and so on.

Obviously your viewpoint depends on your standpoint, but to my mind a lot of the criticism of the press was unfair, and ill-informed as well. I often felt like saying to people who were having a go at me 'OK mate, you come and write it yourself and then ask someone else how fair they think it is.' Every journalist's got a thousand readers with a thousand different ideas about what's fair and what isn't.

The most common criticism was we only reported trouble, incidents like fights between pickets and police, and we ignored all the peaceful side of things. That's a perfectly reasonable comment but it ignores a basic fact of the trade, which is that if something happens it's news, if nothing happens it isn't. 'Man Bites Dog' is news, 'Dog Doesn't Bite Man' isn't news. It might be very exasperating to go on and on reading about incidents day after day outside different pits: but Christ, we were sent out looking to find them, we couldn't come back with no stories. We'd get the wire there was trouble somewhere, or there was going to be: you'd belt off like the clappers and if you got there after it was over, all you could do was go round asking what'd happened. Do that two or three times and your boss began to look at you a bit sideways: to him you seemed to be getting into the habit of being slow off the mark. 'What's the matter son, bed too warm was it, wife didn't know which number to ring you at?'

Or you'd get a tip something was going to happen and you'd go off bloody miles in the pouring rain in the middle of the night, and then when you got there the only demonstration was you and one policeman between you. You couldn't afford not to follow up an anonymous tip if it sounded even faintly kosher: but you knew when you got there to the sort of thing I've been talking about that some joker was sitting back and having a giggle with himself at how much grief he'd given you.

And you were always everyone's enemy. Let anyone know in a pub you were a journalist working for the *Daily Guttersnipe*, and in five minutes you'd have six big blokes backing you up against the bar, telling you you were a lying bastard, capitalist scum, a toad and a hypocrite. After that they'd start getting objectionable. It didn't matter whether it was a strike or a football match, it was all the same: you got spat on for writing about what had happened, and you got spat on for what every other sod'd written about what happened. It was the same with every journalist I knew: if you were on the *Moon* you got blamed for what was in the *Sun*, or if you were on the *Mail* for what appeared in the *Female*. If you were on a local say, you carried the can for what was in every one of the nationals.

But you didn't get any credit for any of the decent stories you did do, and specially not for ones you'd tried to do but which didn't reach the page. I had one story I'd really worked on and worked on: the rumour was going round that the police had their own lads mixing in with the demonstrators, dressed exactly like they were, undercover men taking crafty little pictures of people and getting details about them so they could be identified and nailed. I got together a lot of material on it, and sometimes I went to quite a big risk, because if the police had rumbled me I'd have been right in it. It wasn't quite up to the pitch of Woodward and Bernstein exposing President Nixon at Watergate, but sometimes it began to get to feel a bit like it, specially when it came to meeting someone one night in a multi-storey car park. Anyhow, finally I thought I'd got as much as I was ever going to get, and I took it to my boss and laid it out in front of him. He looked at it for at least a full thirty seconds, then he gathered it up and dropped it in his wastepaper bin. He told me to forget it and go and follow up something that could be printed, not something that'd bring the whole of the effing police force down on our necks.

Another time, on the other side, I did a story which I'd checked and cross-checked with at least six different people, about a certain trades union official who'd accepted some hospitality which he shouldn't have. The man's bosses demanded an immediate retraction and apology from the paper. The point is though that it was true, but it didn't stop the paper issuing a correction and withdrawing it. They'd been told they'd have a walk-out if they didn't. Then the word went out from that particular union

– it wasn't the NUM by the way – that from then on I was to be given no help by anybody on anything else I asked. I was treated with a lot of unhelpfulness by several other people in other unions too, for a long time afterwards. The real thing that bugged me was that the man I'd written about was eventually disciplined by his union for the very thing I'd written about. Nobody gave me an apology or a retraction though, or welcomed me back to the offices with open arms.

I'm not one of those who thinks journalists and reporters are some kind of vultures going round only digging up dirt about people, printing anything that's detrimental, but to only one side, and deliberately painting a false picture. There's only one thing that interests a good journalist, and that's a good story: and most of the ones I know go to immense trouble to get their facts right. Anyone who didn't would soon find himself out of a job. They say that in your career you're allowed one mistake, one misunderstanding and one downright lie: and after that no one'll take you on unless your name's ******, which you'd better not print. To get a story you sometimes have to trample on people's feelings in the sense of ignoring them, but who doesn't do that in their jobs: doctors, dentists, lawyers, policemen. You name them, the list could go on for ever.

I think the strike was misrepresented in some ways not because of deliberate intent, but principally because newspapers try to print what they think their readers want to read. If you look at a Russian newspaper all you see in it's endless reports of speeches and conferences. No one wants to read them and no one does. People want news: and the sad fact is that most news is about violence of one kind or another. If you tried to sell a newspaper entirely on stories about sheep and cows living peacefully in fields with nothing happening all day, you couldn't do it; no one would buy it. But a vicar running off with a choirboy, a motorway pile-up of forty cars, a punch-up between police and pickets, someone killing someone – people'll read all the details you can give them about things like that.

Sometimes I think half their pleasure comes afterwards from turning round and saying how disgusting newspapers are for printing it all.

A lot of people I knew in newspapers in the strike, they were good strong union men themselves: when it came to a choice they were definitely on the side of the miners, their sympathies were entirely with them. I was myself, mine were. Higher up, editorially I mean, obviously it was a different matter. But the actual writers and collectors of news, the scribes themselves, some of them even went so far as believing they were doing the strikers a good turn by reporting how heavy the police were coming on. A chap, a friend of mine did a piece about Nottinghamshire working miners: how much money they were earning because they weren't standing solid with their mates and striking. He wasn't praising them for it, but someone got hold of it up here, and I've more than once had it waved under my nose. First of all as though I'd written it, and secondly as though it was carefully thought out with the deliberate intention of making trouble between strikers and their wives.

I'd say now that all in all I'm glad now to be out of that world. It wasn't a job anybody ever gave you any credit for. You were always at the boss's beck and call day and night, go here go there, there's a story breaking, go and see if there's a story breaking, get it back to us fast, don't get any mistakes in it or you'll be put on the arts page, where the hell have you been, get on over to such a place. And then on the other side your grateful readers: are you the bastard who wrote that snide piece saying Newcastle United's defence was a bit rocky when they lost six–nil, anyone can kick someone when they're down can't they, why didn't you write about the smart new corner flags we've got? After a bit you got very thick-skinned, you had to be or you couldn't survive: all you really thought about was getting the story, getting your copy in and going home to a quiet evening in front of the telly with the wife and kids.

Elaine Houghton, school-leaver

– I'm seventeen. I've had two jobs since I left school, one of them was straight away when I went as an assistant in a cake shop in the next village which my auntie owned. She offered me the job before I left school, she said it would be something for me to do while I made up my mind about other things else. I only worked I think it was two months, because then the shop closed down because she got married again and went to live over at Newcastle. The people who took it on after her were a husband and wife and they didn't want anyone else to help them.

I think I had six or eight months without anything. I kept looking in the newspapers but all there was was part-time work and I wanted to try and get something decent. I went for interview for a couple of jobs but I didn't get them. Then I saw one of the motorway cafés wanted girls. It would have meant being there either for half-past six in the morning on one shift, or till ten o'clock at night on the other and my dad said he wouldn't be happy for me doing it. I think mam felt at least it was something for me, so I went to see the man who was managing it. He told me he'd pick me up in his car at night and bring me home, but to tell the truth I didn't like the look of him very much. I've got my name down now again at the job centre, but I think they don't take you seriously if you're a girl. They think all you've got in mind is getting married, I don't think they make a serious effort to place you anywhere.

I think it's a shame people in this village are having such a worrying time at the present. My dad isn't a miner, he works for one of the garages in Newcastle, he's a mechanic. But I've got two uncles in the pit, and I know both of them don't know what they'll do if the pit's closed. I don't think it's right that when people have worked all their lives for somebody like they've done for the Coal Board, they should find themselves when they get middle-aged being told they can either go to another pit which is perhaps a fair bit away, or take redundancy and be out of work. I'm glad I'm not married to a miner.

I've a boyfriend, he's at technical college studying to be an apprentice electrician. It's a job his father has fixed up for him but I don't know the details of it. He says when he's done all his exams, he doesn't want to stop in this country, he thinks there's lots more opportunity in some place like say Australia. We've talked about it a lot: I can see how someone feels like that, I feel like that myself.

I was born and brought up in Red Hill and all my family live round about. I think the heart will go right out of it if the pit is closed. It's not nice for anybody here nowadays. I know they always say when you look back at your childhood, the sun was always shining and everything you remember as rosy and happy, but I think it was much happier in those days than now. There was much more going on in the village, and I think people had more money then. One thing they did have a lot more was security: they were in jobs and they knew they'd be working next week, next month and next year, which they don't know any more.

I should think my boyfriend and I will definitely get married and go and live somewhere else. I won't want to go on living here with everything grinding down and people having so much poverty. It was awful in the strike, I wish the miners had won. We had a debate about it at school, and about Mr Scargill: it was very interesting and there wasn't anyone in the whole class who didn't feel the miners were right. The teacher said we should have some people putting the other point of view even if they didn't agree with it, because that was what a debate was for, to hear all sides of the question. But there wasn't any other side to the question, there wasn't as far as all the pupils in our class could see it.

Also, I think some of the people in the Government ought to come up here and talk to people and see what they've done to their lives.

Envoi

Three months after these interviews were concluded, the National Coal Board closed Red Hill pit.

Appendices

1 Chronology of events

2 Bibliography

3 Here We Go (For the Women of the Working Class)

Appendix 1   Chronology of events

1981   December   Arthur Scargill elected President of the National Union of Mineworkers (NUM) on a vote of over 70%. (The highest ever recorded.)

1983   March   Ian MacGregor, former Chairman of British Steel Corporation, announced as next Chairman of the National Coal Board (NCB). His previous employers were paid compensation of £1½m ('transfer fee') for his loss.

NCB South Yorkshire Area Director tells Cortonwood (Yorkshire) miners their pit will be kept open for 'at least five to six years'. Pledge repeated a month later.

April   NUM moved its Headquarters to Sheffield.

June   Mrs Thatcher and the Conservatives won third General Election in succession, with a landslide majority of 144.

September   Ian MacGregor began work as NCB Chairman.

1984 January   NCB announce new policy to reduce production capacity 'in the near future', offering higher redundancy payments. Arthur Scargill described it as 'a recipe for disaster'.

March   NCB announce Cortonwood Colliery, near Sheffield, to be closed in one month's time.

Strikes begin. An NOP poll says 51% of miners would vote for a strike and 34% against it.

May   First meeting between Ian MacGregor and Arthur Scargill since the beginning of the dispute. It lasts sixty minutes and is described by Scargill as 'a fiasco'.

July   Chancellor Nigel Lawson announces that so far between £300m and £350m has been spent on the strike: and that 'even in narrow financial terms it represents a worthwhile investment for the nation'.

August   At a pit in Yorkshire 1,000 police escort one miner back to work.

In Durham, police battle for five days with pickets to get one man into a colliery.

1985 January   City financial analysts say the strike is costing over £85m per week.

February   Arrests of strikers and pickets so far total more than 10,000.

Large numbers of miners begin to abandon the strike. The NCB claims over 50% are working.

March A Delegate Conference at the TUC votes by 98 to 91 to end the strike and return to work.

Appendix 2   Bibliography

Artworker Books, *Blood, Sweat & Tears: photographs from the Great Miners' Strike*, 1985.

Atkinson, G. L., *Collieries in Northumberland and Durham*, NCB, 1980.

Beynon, Huw (ed.), *Digging Deeper: Issues in the Miners' Strike*, Verso, 1985.

Fraser, Kit, *Toff Down Pit*, Quartet, 1984.

Garside, W. R., *The Durham Miners 1919–1960*, Allen & Unwin, 1971.

Glyn, Andrew, *The Economic Case Against Pit Closures*, NUM, 1985.

Goodman, Geoffrey, *The Miners' Strike*, Pluto Press, 1985.

Heroes (LP), Consett Music Project, 1985.

Kendal, Stephen, 'The Mining Strike of 1984/5: A personal view', for private circulation, 1985.

Lloyd, John, *Understanding the Miners' Strike*, Fabian Society, 1985.

McHugh, Phil, *Unfinished Business*, Coppice Press, 1985.

Northumberland Miners' Union, *Centenary Brochure 1863–1963*.

Pattison, K. and Beynon, H., *Easington August '84*, Side Publications, 1985.

Reed, David and Adamson, Olivia, *Miners' Strike 1984–1985: People Versus State*, Larkin Publications, 1985.

Stephenson, John, *The Pit People*, privately printed, 1985.

Walker, Peter, Review of Geoffrey Goodman's *The Miners' Strike* in the *Sunday Times*, October 1985.

Which Side Are You On (LP), Music for the Miners from the North East, Which Side Records, 1985.

Wilsher, P., Macintyre, D. and Jones, M., *Strike*, Coronet Books, 1985.

Woolf, Emile, 'Digging Holes in the NCB's Accounts', article in the *Guardian*, July 1985.

Work and Employment Research Unit, University of Durham, '(Mis)Managing Horden', 1985.

Worsborough Community Group, *The Heart and Soul Of It*, Bannerworks, 1985.

Appendix 3 Here we Go (For the Women of the Working Class)

You are women you are strong you are fighting for your
lives
Side by side with your men who work the nation's mines
United by the struggle united by the past
And it's here we go here we go for the women of the
working class

You don't need Government's approval for anything you
do
You don't need their permission to have a point of view
You don't need anyone to tell you what to think or say
You've strength enough and wisdom of your own to go
your own way
You are women you are strong you are fighting for your
lives

They talk about statistics about the price of coal
The cost is your community it's dying on the dole
In fighting for your future you've found ways to organise
Where Women's Liberation failed to move this strike has
mobilised
You are women you are strong you are fighting for your
lives

Yours is a unity that threats can never breach
Yours an education books or schools could never teach
You face the taunts and the violence of Thatcher's thugs
in blue

When you're fighting for survival you've got nothing left
to lose

You are women you are strong you are fighting for your
lives
Side by side with your men who work the nation's mines
United by the struggle united by the past
And it's here we go here we go for the women of the
working class
And it's here we go here we go for the women of the
working class

Words and music copyright by Mal Finch, 1985.

Acknowledgments

In the 1939–45 war I was a conscientious objector, and when I appeared in front of a tribunal in Manchester I was given exemption from military service on condition that I worked on the land, or in civil defence, coal mining or the Fire Service. I chose coal mining, thinking it would be an experience I'd otherwise never be likely to have, coming as I did from a conventional middle-class background and having been educated at a public school.

I was quite right. For eighteen months I worked in a now-closed pit in the Lancashire coalfield, and lived and worked among miners and their families until I was injured in an accident underground and subsequently discharged on medical grounds. That experience of being in a mining community, and working (however inefficiently and ineptly) among coal miners, was one which radically changed my outlook, my political attitude, and my awareness – or, rather, my previous lack of it – of the class-based nature of our society, and particularly of how the materially poor and educationally underprivileged are always at the mercy of the wealthy, the comfortable, and the frequently uncaring. I also became gradually aware of the deep-running and deeply-imbued mystique of coal mining to those involved in it, of the strength of the bonds between miners and mining families, and of how being able to say 'I'm a coal miner', 'I'm the wife of a coal miner', or 'My father was a coal miner' carries a cachet of specialness and pride. The after-effects of my brief connection with the industry have lasted ever since: and in every subsequent dispute between miners and the Government, of whatever political persuasion it was, my sympathies have always been immediately and unshakeably with the miners. I was intrigued to read forty years later in Kit Fraser's splendid book *Toff Down Pit*, which I was reviewing for *New Society*, that he too had had the same residual feelings as I did after he'd worked in a coal mine.

So my first and fundamental acknowledgment is to those men I worked among in a pit so long ago, for illuminating for me some of the feeling of what it's actually like to be a miner. Without that experience, I think it's unlikely I'd ever have known, or much cared, about this historically rich and dignified sector of British industry, or of the importance of trades unionism in the betterment of social conditions and education. And therefore during the miners' strike of 1984–5 in common with many other people – half or more of the population probably – I was shocked and appalled by the then Conservative Government's ruthless and devious attempts to divide the country, crush the spirit of the miners, break the power of the National Union of Mineworkers, and destroy the popularity of its President, Arthur Scargill.

Some months after the strike had finished, when the miners had been driven back to work and the Government had 'won', I approached the NUM and asked their help in putting together a book of interviews with members of a mining community whose pit was in the shadow of the threat of closure. I was not very optimistic about being given it, particularly as I'd just read a book by the distinguished industrial editor of a well-known daily newspaper, in which he said that while he was writing it the National Union of Mineworkers 'treated me with great courtesy . . . [but] decided against co-operating with any authorship outside the NUM'. I did not disclose to anyone either my political sympathies, or the fact that years ago I'd worked in a coal mine myself, as both seemed somewhat weakly irrelevant. All I had to work with was a slight Lancashire accent, a copy of a previous book I'd done, and the idea for this new book which I'd pinched from the photographer Fay Godwin. But I was immediately warmly welcomed, and the Union's Secretary Peter Heathfield made it possible for me to have the advice and assistance of Dave Feickert, their Research Officer in Sheffield. He in turn went to considerable trouble to give me information and introductions: and in a short time I was privileged to meet and talk at length with Jack Collins, Kent Area Secretary of the NUM, Sam Scott the Secretary of the Northumberland Area, and Bill Dowding, Research Officer at Red Hill, the Headquarters of the Durham Area. All three were endlessly helpful, throughout a time which was extremely busy and worrying for them. I am most grateful for their unstinting assistance and the unrestricted facilities they provided: without them my book most certainly couldn't have been written.

Many other people in the NUM also helped me. It is sad that because of the atmosphere of unease and distrust which now exists between the Union and the National Coal Board, for very good reasons they have asked me not to mention their names or specify exactly what they did for me. It's only fair to say too, and perhaps it should be emphasised, that a number of employees of the National Coal Board, at management level, were willing to talk and record long interviews with me, though again on condition their names wouldn't be used and they should be given protective anonymity. And additionally I can and do thank Brian Williams, Ervin Lyons, Alec Turner, Bill Crosby, Edith and Tommy Scholick, Gerald Wilson, Juliana Heron, Christine Ward, Stephen Kendal, Jan and Peter Smith, and Anne Suddick: they all answered interminable questions and helped in innumerable ways, as well as introducing me to people with differing views and experiences, even though in some cases it meant they had to swallow strong personal feelings of antipathy towards them, in order that I could get a fairer picture. Huw Beynon, Reader in Sociology at the University of Durham, was also greatly helpful, as was his colleague Linda Nurse.

Again and as usual Genevieve Broad swiftly and accurately typed and retyped numerous drafts and the final manuscript, and at great cost in time and trouble Vivian Broad repeatedly delivered and collected material for me. Myra Perring of Group Management Services made and expertly collated photocopies, giving generously of her own free time to do it. My agent Gill Coleridge of Anthony Sheil Associates encouraged, calmed and cosseted me; and David Godwin my editor at Heinemann was always enthusiastically supportive. I thank them all: as I do once again my wife Margery, as ever, for her help and love.

Tony Parker
Good Friday, 1986
Westleton, Suffolk

TONY PARKER

SOLDIER, SOLDIER

Soldier, Soldier is perhaps the most truthful and fascinating book yet written about modern British soldiers. Tony Parker, a writer with an unequalled gift for empathy and social observation, was given almost unlimited facilities by the Ministry of Defence and spent eighteen months interviewing the officers and men of one infantry regiment.

Soldier, Soldier is an honest and frank account of what it is like to be a soldier, or the wife of one, in the Army of today.

'A book so gripping that I sat up reading it far into the night. A unique and revealing glimpse into the lives and thoughts of the men in khaki. Anyone reading this brilliant book will never look at our servicemen in the same way again'
Gerald Kaufman in the Manchester Evening News

A Royal Mail service in association with the Book Marketing Council & The Booksellers Association.
Post-A-Book is a Post Office trademark

ANTHONY KEMP

THE SECRET HUNTERS

'Missing in Action.'

That was the official line. World War Two was over, Germany was in chaos and the British authorities preferred not to stir up more trouble – or make more work for themselves.

But the British SAS and Special Operations men – and women – were not 'missing in action'. They had been killed: shot as saboteurs on Hitler's orders or murdered in concentration camps.

The Secret Hunters is the story of how a small, dedicated group of their ex-comrades refused to accept that official line. Starting with a suppressed report into the horrors of the Nazi camps, they searched relentlessly for the truth, uncovering the grisly evidence and tracking down the war criminals responsible: the men who gave the orders, who pulled the triggers and operated the gas chambers.

CORONET BOOKS

HENRY HAMMAN AND STUART PARROTT

MAYDAY AT CHERNOBYL

On April 26th, 1986 at 1.23 a.m. an accident
occurred that changed nuclear history.

Mayday At Chernobyl tells the story of the world's
worst nuclear disaster – why and how it happened –
using Soviet and Western sources.

* Did the Soviet Union try to hide the truth about
  Chernobyl?
* How many people will die of cancer because of
  the Chernobyl disaster?
* Can the environment recover?
* Why did some Western governments cover up
  the facts about fallout from Chernobyl?

Mayday At Chernobyl puts the whole Chernobyl
accident into context, shows how it will affect one
of the world's superpowers and how both East and
West used the accident for their own political ends.

NEW ENGLISH LIBRARY

ALSO AVAILABLE FROM
HODDER AND STOUGHTON PAPERBACKS